THE STANDOUT LEADER

Discover ways of leaving your mark

DEEPAK MOHLA

STARDOM BOOKS

www.StardomBooks.com

STARDOM BOOKS, LLC
112, Bordeaux Ct, Coppell,
TX 75019

FIRST EDITION OCTOBER 2023

STARDOM BOOKS

A Division of Stardom Alliance
112, Bordeaux Ct, Coppell, TX
75019 www.stardombooks.com

Stardom Books, United States Stardom Books, India

THE STANDOUT LEADER

Deepak Mohla

p. 190

cm. 13.5 X 21.5

Category:
BUS071000   BUSINESS & ECONOMICS / Leadership
SEL027000   SELF-HELP / Personal Growth / Success

ISBN: 978-1-957456-29-4

DEDICATION

The forebearers who built the legacy we have.

Om Parkash & Savitri Mohla

To posterity, who would build on the legacy we leave.

Kavir, Vedansh & Sitar

CONTENTS

ACKNOWLEDGMENTS

This book would not have been initiated without the prodding of the Publisher, Raam Anand, who convinced me that I have not one, but countless stories to narrate.

Writing the book has taken me down memory lane and I appreciate the debt of gratitude I owe to my mentors, bosses and associates who made an ordinary person reach levels that would not have been deemed possible by anyone.

To Prof. Abad Ahmad, my Guru, who made a huge impact not only during the early days of my career, but also in my later years— His humility and clarity of thought has always been inspiring.

My gratitude to all my bosses who had a massive hand in giving me the independence that I always needed to thrive— Anantharaman, Zareer Kapadia, Dhun Gandhi, Shanti Roy, Madan Agarwal, Madan Mehta.

A fond remembrance to Rajan Nanda who did not allow my ego to get the better of me; and to Karl Kummer, who helped me develop a global perspective and backed me to follow my instincts!

Special thanks to Dr. B.K. Modi who had presented me with a huge canvas to paint on. He had given me the freedom to fail, learn and lead. He always believed in me and trusted my passions. It is from him that I have imparted the idea of "think beyond your horizon" and be aware of what to avoid. I cannot thank Mr. K.L. Chugh enough for mentoring my transition from Corporate to Consulting.

Had I not connected with Claus Moeller, Kostas & Prof. Tony Cockerill, I would not have opened the door to my inner-self and figured out my purpose. Hence, a deep sense of gratitude for them.

Everything that I have learnt so far has been to a large extent due to my endless arguments and discussions with colleagues who became lifelong friends. I take the risk of naming a few but know that the ones I refuse to name would indulge me– Vivek, Hardeep,

Palani, Dhruv, Arun Gupta, Deepak Talwar, Prakash, Umang, Arun Kapur, Deepak Kapur, Naresh, Suresh and so on.

I am thankful to the band of Brothers & Sister (BOBS) - Bernward, George, Octavian, Vicky & Jens. With them, every conversation has been an insightful experience.

To all my business associates, dealers, vendors, business partners — Without you, I would not have learnt what FMS did not have in its curriculum; the practical business!

Khurshid Bandyopadhyay has been a guardian angel and the repository of numerous stories and human insights. I have learnt the art of being firm with one's ideals from her.

Thanks to my colleague Arzoo in helping me with the drafting of the book & to the editing team of Rekha, Sthitodhi & Sandipta for their diligence, constant support and exhortation. Thank you Tejas for helping with the cover design!

A huge dollop of credit for this book goes to my colleague & friend Suman, who has had my back for over twenty-five years. She has been the super-editor for this book. I'm also grateful to Lekha Mukherjee, my friend, for taking her precious time in editing the book.

Thanks to Karan, Pia, Kartik, and Amrita for providing me with the window to witness and understand the aspirations of today's youth!

A business partnership between a husband & wife is expected to fall apart sooner than later. Well, either the business or the marriage. My immense sense of indebtedness to Neeta. We ran the business for over twenty-five years and the marriage for over forty years, which is still going strong and brimming with joy. Thankyou Neeta for being the inspiration and unsparing critic of several ideas. The writing of this book would not have been possible without your support.

FOREWORD

The book **"The Standout Leader"** authored by Deepak Mohla is based on his rich experiences from his career as a Management Trainee to the top echelons of organisations, coupled with his equally rich experience in the Leadership Development and Consulting domain. The author has developed a strong conviction based on his experiences and that of others with whom he consulted that **ordinary people can and do create extraordinary results**. This strong belief motivated the author to share these experiences with others and inspire them to believe in themselves and achieve standout performance.

The book is targeted towards young emerging leaders who have been performing junior /mid-management roles over a period and are at the cusp of their career where the next step can take them into the orbit of a Leadership role. The book helps young Managers to standout at every career turn and become a standout leader by developing a path for themselves of self-discovery, purpose, building self-confidence through working on self-development plans, etc. The book focuses on how to maximise every career turn and inspire yourself to standout at every opportunity.

The Standout Leader creates a narrative through enlightening experiences and stories that are highly readable and easy to grasp. With simple practical ideas and many examples, the book leads the reader on the critical role that clarity of PURPOSE can have on the careers of men & women. It takes the reader through the process of self-awareness and self-discovery; to understand one's ability to create value; what are an individual's motivators; what are a person's development needs. Understanding one's strengths and development areas helps a person to face each challenge with confidence and convert crisis to opportunity. Knowing yourself is like having an armoury and the knowledge how to use different arrows in a given situation to gain maximum advantage. What are the various tools and methodologies you can use to get to know yourself? How to create a personal development plan with the help of Leadership Capability Canvas?

The book shares the importance of learning on the job through many examples, based on the experiences of various leaders— How learning is a process of taking action, analysing the impact of that action, of receiving feedback and the process of self-reflection. The author shares and explains the High-Performance Behaviours which are crucial for Leaders to be successful in a VUCAD world. The importance of learning agility (Innovating, Performing, Reflecting, Risking). Knowing what is adaptability and risk-taking and how this one capability helps catapult leaders into a different orbit.

One of the most critical roles of a leader is managing teams & people. The author extensively deals with the subject by using examples interspersed with simple frameworks e.g. the Vitality Curve. The book discusses the importance of the leader in having self-belief; leading disruptive change; building trust with team members; empowering and delegating; reviewing performance; feedback & coaching; and making people succeed.

On disruptive change the author discusses how a leader need not shy away from risk taking- Bigger the risk, bigger the gains. For standout leaders, incremental approach is mediocrity. growth only happens with challenges. Bigger the platform, higher the chances of being catapulted to next levels of learning and growth.

The author identifies the critical capabilities required to jump the curve from team leader to leader of a leader. Again, with many examples, the book focuses on the aspect of Alignment, Collaboration and Teamwork. The book discusses how conflicts emerge and how leaders must learn to deal with conflicts and toxicity in the workplace.

The author draws on the concept of 'Teamship', and how to build a healthy team; role of the leader in developing leaders; the characteristics of winning teams; and how to deal with toxicity and dysfunctionality in teams. In the last chapter, the author focuses on one of the most critical aspects of Leadership- **Building your Power Grid.**

The author introduces the framework of 4Ps: Performance, Personal Brand and Positive relationships built on the behaviours of empathy, persuasion and self-confidence. How it is vital for leaders to create a personal brand, how performance is an essential factor but not sufficient for the personal brand, the ability to build a network of positive relationships over time both within and outside your organisation would determine the success of your purpose.

The author strongly emphasises the behaviour of listening and compassion. Empathy is one of the most critical elements of High-performance behaviours and is non-negotiable if a person is to succeed in a leadership role.

The Standout Leader is replete with deep insights and various practical examples. It is an easy read with its conversational approach. For emerging young leaders, it would provide many answers to their questions in a fast-changing world.

I find **'The Standout Leader'** as an exciting, unconventional, inspiring, and practical book. I am sure it would provide inspiration to the young leaders who wish to leave their mark in this world.

Prof Abad Ahmad

Former Dean, Faculty of Management (FMS),
Former Pro-Vice Chancellor, University of Delhi.
Former Chairman, Aga Khan Foundation (India).

INTRODUCTION

"Books are mirrors: you only see in them what you already have inside you."

— *Carlos Ruiz Zafón, The Shadow of the Wind*

Out of all the skills that an individual must possess, reading should undoubtedly be one of them. Reading books provides an unparalleled opportunity to build an extensive vocabulary, broaden our horizons of knowledge, and shape our minds to mould ourselves into a better version of us. I developed an intense passion for reading in my pre-teens, which continued late into my professional life. I call it an intense passion because I would require something to read mandatorily, at every opportunity— be it eating, my morning rituals, getting ready for school, travelling, before sleeping, after waking up, etc. I barely recall a day when I failed to lay my hands on a book. Reading helped me to calm my chaos and mirror my hidden spirit to strive for the best.

One of my sister's friends was a novelist. She would mostly write romantic novels. One day, I was so immersed in her book while eating that I accidentally stained some of the pages with oily turmeric marks. I guess that qualifies me as a serious reader since most avid readers in India would have turmeric marks on some of the books they have read! On the other end of the spectrum, religious texts also held me in rapturing attention– I perhaps read the scriptures eight to ten times. Albeit it was always for the stories in them, and not for any spiritual or religious purposes.

There are certain authors who stay with us even if it has been years since we may have touched or got a glance of their books. There is a tug at our heartstrings whenever we recall those notable authors and their creations. One such author, for me, was Nevil Shute. He left an indelible mark on the impressionable persona of my pre-teens. I believe I would have read most of his books, if not all, in a short period of time. His books were an addition to a sea of other books I would read simultaneously.

I often wondered what it was about Nevil Shute's stories that impacted me so strongly. I think what was remarkable in his stories were that the heroes and heroines were ordinary people. If given a situation, they would do extraordinary things and make a life-changing difference to those around them. One of his books, *A Town Like Alice*, based on actual events, brought vividly to life the characters so ordinary, yet so extraordinary in their impact.

What caught my attention was how despite being ordinary people, they fought every battle and stood out as leaders. Since time immemorial, ordinary people have always been ignored, yet they are the ones who often do extraordinary things. They may be belittled and considered unworthy, yet they end up surprising everyone with their metamorphosis. Hence, I vehemently stand by Alan Turing's words, *"Sometimes it is the people no one can imagine anything of who do the things no one can imagine."*

Around that time an epiphany struck me that if they could overcome every barrier on their journey, so could I. I could see who I wanted to be and A Town Like Alice mirrored my vision of standing out from the crowd. That was when I knew it could be possible for me, an ordinary man, to stand out and be counted for the extraordinary deeds I might perform when faced with a particular situation.

People find it very convenient to blame their circumstances or others, if they do not fare well in life. After all, it requires no effort to condemn one's surroundings rather than take responsibility in trying to overcome the hurdles. In my opinion, every individual should make the most out of the limited resources they possess instead of whining about what they do not have. The magic in Nevil Shute's stories unknowingly had a significant impact in creating a belief that I must utilise every opportunity bestowed upon me. A penchant for opting for the road less travelled by, as Robert Frost suggests, evolved in me creating a sense of adventure and helping me embark on new paths.

This perspective burnt away the feeling that I was not good enough to try new-fangled, and often norm-defying ideas. It brought forth the belief and self-confidence that I do not require to be superhuman to make an impact. The halo I had created in my imagination around people with extraordinary powers got significantly diluted. Being an average student or performer in the social circuit was no longer an excuse not to punch above my weight. What was important was how I took charge of the numerous opportunities that life threw at me. This attitude instinctively helped me to set challenges for myself almost every day.

For five years, I travelled in the University special bus from Sujan Singh Park to Maurice Nagar with people of my milieu, social strata and background. Possibly, a lot of people at that stage of their education and careers would leave a strong imprint in their future. I often recognise a few of those faces today from the electronic and other media— social and print. Some of them have developed into remarkable leaders— standing out from the group.

I started my career in a batch of twelve management trainees from a similar background— mostly MBAs from premier institutions. Today, a few decades later, some have created institutions and become entrepreneurs, while a few stumbled by the wayside succumbing to the umpteen challenges they encountered. MBAs or non-MBAs made no difference in how these people evolved. The distinguishing factor was how they utilised the opportunities that came on their way with courage, hope and persistence when they battled the challenges that arrived as a barrier to their goals. Not all of them were clear about what they wanted, but the desire to LEAVE A MARK - TO STAND OUT FROM THE CROWD was inherent in them.

Man on a Mission

A few years ago, my consulting firm received an unusual request. Well, it was unusual because the person for whom the request was being made was the patriarch of a large conglomerate in the infrastructure sector. Besides this, even the nature of the proposal was unusual. He wanted us to conduct a workshop on "Time Management" for his family (the promoters) and some of the senior leaders of the group.

Our firm conducts several leadership development interventions at different levels. Time Management and the ability to prioritise is one such intervention. However, it is typically a capability that one is expected to develop by the time you have taken your first managerial role. We were taken aback seeing a workshop on Time Management being prioritised during this time in their careers. All the intended participants were at senior leadership positions. My colleague and I agreed to attend the workshop as our curiosity was sufficiently piqued. As usual, for a workshop to begin at 9:30 am, we reached our client's office at around 8 am so that we had enough time to set up the technology and ensure the conference room set-up was consistent with our plans that were sent earlier.

By 8:30 am, when we were almost ready, the patriarch entered the conference room. I recognised him from his pictures in the media and introduced my colleague and myself. He graciously invited us to his office. We thought it would be good to understand from him– why was there any need for a time management workshop at this level? When we asked him why, he gave us an enigmatic smile and said, "You'll get to know within a couple of hours."

We conversed with him for a few minutes; by then, it was about 9:15 am. We took his leave mentioning that we would go to the conference room to meet the senior executives/members of the promoter family, who were to participate, before we started the workshop. He mentioned that he would join us as soon as we were ready to begin. When we entered the conference room, we found out that only the HR Head of the group and a couple of CEOs from the operating companies had arrived. As we exchanged conversations with them while waiting for the others to join, we learned from the HR head that the group for the workshop consisted often to eleven participants-six members of the family (the Chairman, his two sons, a son-in-law and his brother-in-law) and five professionals, out of which only 3 had already arrived.

Since it was almost 9:45 am, there was a dire need to connect with the missing members and check when we could expect them. At around 10 am, the Chairman made a brief entry and observed that the participants were yet to arrive, so he advised us to call him when everyone was present. Frantic efforts to connect with the errant family members and create a quorum by getting a few executives to attend the workshop appeared futile. We were awkward, embarrassed and perturbed at what had transpired. We felt hugely disrespected that we had come all the way to conduct the session, and our time was treated with disdain as if it did not matter and we were insignificant.

Finally, after a long time, a quorum was formed with only one son, one son-in-law, and the brother-in-law, along with four executives from the original plan and three executives who were hustled in as last-minute fill-ins. The people missing in action were— one son and one CEO from the initial list of participants. We started the session at 11:45 am against the scheduled time of 9:30 am. Besides the Chairman, 2 CEOs, and the group HR head, all the others were late— ranging from 60 mins to 140 mins! It was immensely annoying and disrespectful. When we started the session, the Chairman asked us, "Have you learned the answer to your question of why we needed a session on "Time Management" for the senior most team of our group?" As we progressed through the session, it was evident that the issues were not of planning their time and being organised, but the attitude and mindset of not valuing time as the most critical and perishable resource.

The central learning for me was the role of the Chairman and how he identified the most critical issue. The appropriate attitude and mindset of the leaders are crucial if businesses and institutions need to be created. An entrepreneurial zeal and passion are necessary for creation, innovation and green field projects. Being born into a privileged family holds no guarantee for success. An entrepreneur recognises the criticality of time and tide (business opportunities in the case of this group). A leader is also an opportunist in terms of identifying opportunities before others do, which distinguishes pioneers from followers. For the Chairman, it was mandatory to give this message in the most telling way possible to his family. He delivered the message with aplomb, using us as the messenger.

That was the day I realised why the patriarch was such a successful entrepreneur, a leader who created one of the largest infrastructure groups in the country and a man on a mission. He had comprehended that the biggest bottleneck to growth could be the family unless they were committed to the growth story. He also identified that a critical change in their attitude and behaviour was required for them to become a part of the growth story and subsequently lead it. He believed that in order to achieve remarkable goals, he must have a close backup of his family, friends and community. If there was no alignment with them in terms of direction and commitment, he would not be able to maximise his opportunity of making the most out of everything.

He had a dire messianic zeal incumbent of an entrepreneur and the desire to demand and nourish the same passion, behaviour and attitude within his family and leadership team. To create a movement that could help him achieve his goals, he extended the concept of family to his village and to his larger community. There was no false humility but an explicit acceptance of being a man on a mission with a clear sense of purpose.

The Extra Step

As a manager, one consistent feedback I have derived from my team members is that I am 'difficult to please'. Even if they achieved their goals, they would seldom get a rating from me that was above a B (*on a scale of A-D, with D being lowest*) or a rating above a 3 (*on a scale of 1-5, with 1 being lowest*).

As a young manager, I could perhaps not communicate properly to my team members what they needed to do to achieve the highest levels of performance– Level 5 or Level A. I knew instinctively that while they had achieved the goals, something was lacking that held me back from granting them the highest rating. In my initial years as a manager, performance reviews would sometimes be a nerve-wracking experience.

I was convinced that there was a great degree of headroom available to the team members to improve their performance beyond what they had accomplished. However, instead of explaining why the rating was low, I found it more rewarding to help them understand what additional opportunities they could have utilised to do even better. We often set goals for ourselves and are thrilled when we attain them. Some organisations have lucrative bonuses and incentives for fulfilling performance goals at all levels. Hence, if I miss my target, it is not only my bonus that may be impacted but that of my boss too. Inevitably, an environment of risk aversion sets in the organisation, leading to a level 3 performance.

As I progressed in understanding leadership behaviours, I could clearly visualise and articulate what a level 5 performance could be for a person in different situations. A level 5 performance outlives the person in the organisation. Even when the person has moved on, the performance, the actions, and the impact continue as a part of the organisation's way of working and the legends around which the brand and culture evolve.

A story was narrated by a senior leader of an organisation that is a global player in the elevator industry. He shared how a team was way behind in installing an escalator at the launch of a metro station. The launch was to herald the commencement of the metro system in the Indian capital city. The delays were partially in control of the installation and commissioning team, but that was of no consideration to the entire team. The company brand was involved, and the team was staring at the horror of a potential headline the next day 'Metro launch delayed due to the ineptitude of XYZ company.'

The leader told me he was a Project Manager and under massive pressure. His director, who was in charge of all installations, camped in the city for a week and helped him coordinate with all agencies within the logistics company, the customer's departments and the other vendors. In addition, he focused on keeping the team morale high. Delay was not an option discussed at all. Finally, the team worked non-stop for thirty-six hours and completed the installation at 6 am– just in time for the inauguration scheduled at noon the same day. The Director became a larger-than-life persona, as did the Project Manager. The team associated with the project became a part of folklore. A legacy was created! *A level 5 performance indeed! The narratives highlight that ordinariness with a purpose, a sense of being on a mission, and extraordinary leadership actions, when knit together, can catapult a leader into being a standout leader!*

Over the years, I have observed my colleagues, managers and leaders who performed at exceptional levels. As a consultant, I also had the advantage of witnessing leaders at different levels in an organisation perform remarkably at times. Many of those leaders had their roots in ordinary middle-class backgrounds. So, the question is– what made these ordinary people perform exceptionally in a leadership role? What went into making these people stand out as leaders?

This book is an endeavour to share my thoughts on what goes into the making and development of these standout leaders. These thoughts are based on my experiences, narratives from colleagues and friends, and observations spread over my long innings in the corporate world and consulting field.

The Evolution of a Standout Leader

Who is a Standout Leader?

This book has been put together for the young leaders who are in their first or second role as Managers, i.e., Managers who are leading teams of individual contributors (IC) and Managers who are guiding teams of Managers who are leading IC teams. The leaders at this stage are facing situations that put them at crossroads of either taking the difficult road of being alone in an adventure, possible failure, many opportunities, and no benchmarks or taking the road well-travelled to security, fewer risks, a somewhat assured career path, and a comfortable future, etc. The Standout Leader focuses on the elements that helped ordinary young men and women to emerge as 'standout' leaders.

The critical elements are:

- **The Essence of Me** – discovering a sharp sense of purpose which can help identify opportunities and sometimes even create opportunities.

- **Discover to Empower** – being aware of your being – what are your strengths and limitations - having a strong sense of self-worth and self-belief.

- **Life is a Lab** – Focusing on continuous reflection-based self-development.

- **Life is a Lab – Leadership Transition**

  o Inspiring others to achieve their potential.
  o Continuously aligning all stakeholders to goals, strategies, actions and results.
  o Collaborating despite barriers for the larger goal. Thinking and acting as 'WE' and not ' I '.

- **Building your Power Grid**

  o Performance, performance, and performance.
  o Creating and living your personal brand.
  o Developing vital leadership traits of empathy, persuasion and self-confidence.

In the subsequent chapters, the book explores these areas through the real-life experiences of many standout leaders.

1

ESSENCE OF ME
A SHARP SENSE OF PURPOSE

I remember witnessing the Republic Day parade on a cold foggy day amidst a vast sea of people. As a child, I was very much in awe of the smartly turned-out armed forces personnel directing people to their respective seats. When the parade started, I was transported into a different world. The smartly turned-out parade of the Army, Air Force, Navy, and even the Girl Guides and Boy Scouts was highly inspiring to a young boy, who was barely four years old. The colourful bands of different services of the armed forces followed the marching units.

I was mesmerised by the music and melody, the unison and harmony of various instruments, and most notably, the bandmaster leading the band. The bandmaster was the leader of the band unit, and the way he marched and led the crew made me stand up with my mouth agape. I got metaphorically transported into a different world. The incident made me involuntarily clap my hands in glee. I was dumbstruck and stunned for a while.

Leadership is the ability to influence a group of people to achieve the desired goal. When a leader harnesses the unique power of their team members, they enable them to achieve leadership excellence too. The bandmaster, at that very moment, became my idol! I thought I would give up anything to become a person of this stature. At times, I wonder if the sharp imprint that the event created on my mind became the precursor to my understanding of who a 'leader' is.

The bandmaster ignited a desire within me to inspire people and lead them gracefully. My vision of a leader evolved into a benevolent, exacting, nurturing, and imposing presence. The bandmaster marshalled very visibly from the front. His directions to his team were simple and straightforward. He led the team members in harmony and in unison with each other and created an excellent environment– a product of his team's efforts for us, the audience/his customers! The bandmaster knew what he wanted his customers to experience and how he should deliver that experience. His unit was well-trained to provide that customer experience. Every team member knew their role to perfection and the context of their position to the other team members.

The imagery was vivid and intense; he became my superhero. I began to connect situations in life with how my superhero would have dealt with that situation. I perceived his impact on me in the audience, even as a four-year-old. As I grew up from childhood to youth to adulthood, that imagery got transferred to different people who impacted me similarly; my father, my teacher in middle school, the cricket team captain in school, and many others who became my heroes– my leaders.

They led from the front, nurtured yet challenged me at every turn, with new problems to be solved and new learnings to be imbibed. They often scolded me, yet I was assured they were on my side. They encouraged me to team up with others. They reviewed my progress, celebrated my successes, and coaxed me out of my failures. They helped me to articulate my dreams so vividly that the actualisation of those dreams did not appear too distant. They also gave me the confidence to take risks as an inherent step towards growth. These were my role models – my 'standout' leaders. A few decades later, a close friend and his family visited us. Their son, Ravi, was a young lad of twelve years of age. He brought a copy of the 'Times of India' and said, "Uncle, I would like you to read this."

The Team Leader helps everyone to achieve success

It was a letter written by Ravi published in the section - notes to the Editor of the newspaper. In that letter, he had shared his unhappiness and angst towards a newspaper report about a mishap that had taken place in the city. He could effectively communicate his feelings on the perpetuated wrongdoing without bringing too much flourish in his writing style or using fancy vocabulary. He had also shared what he felt should be done to alleviate the suffering of the people involved in that episode.

Ravi's feelings of compassion and empathy were so real and evocative that I was assured this young lad would go on to become a public figure and a leader. What resonated with me immediately was Ravi's vision and the innate compassion he felt for his fellow beings. His passion for the cause entirely consumed him. The courage of his conviction was most inspiring, and I hoped it would not get diluted at the altar of pragmatism. Even at that early age, his uncluttered mind and clarity were compelling.

It was no surprise that Ravi got scholarships to study at Cambridge University, UK, and the Kennedy School of Governance & Public Affairs at Harvard over the next decade. He continued his focus on the social sector and worked with different governments on the environment and climate. Today, his views on the subject are sought by most leading investors when they wish to make a significant investment in any project from the environmental, social, and climatic perspectives.

Ravi had discovered his purpose and raison d'être early in life— creating, defending and sustaining a viable co-existence between man and his environment. This calling continued to inspire him, and he pursued it with passion. In the process, he continues to add immense value to society. I believe that Ravi may have moved in a different trajectory and direction if his purpose was not so clear to him at a very young age. That passion was infused with action, and its impact was created on a magnificent number of people.

So, the question is— Why is it essential to have a purpose in life? Do you want it to matter to the people you live with? Do you want your being to matter to people outside your family, extended family, workplace, industry, or city? It would be best if one reflected on the necessity of having a purpose in life. How would having a purpose in life make you a standout leader and a contributing member of society? How would it contribute to your happiness and success in life?

There have been many situations in my life where I felt emotionally drained and nothing seemed to make me feel good and positive. I am sure this has happened with you and most people. There would have been situations when the vicissitudes of life have struck and made you feel helpless. At times like these, having a purpose can be your strategy to pick yourself out of that situation, recharge and refocus your energy.

As you skim through the chapters, you will see that I have spoken about a situation where I felt that my decision to change jobs were wrong. I was struck with a severe cardiological condition at forty-one. During situations like these, we think it is not happening to us; we try to escape our mind's labyrinth, and flee from the chaos, but the truth is, it is happening, and it is happening to us. When we face the realities around us, we either succumb to the situation or fight our way out of it. In the end, we are obligated to face our issues. There is no running away. These are times when manifestations of depression could start appearing if we choose to let the events overwhelm us. Of course, there is help and support from family, friends, and well-wishers. But external resources can never outweigh our internal resilience and hope. A clear purpose, even if not for the long term, can help us overcome these challenging times. During times of crisis like COVID-19, a clear purpose helped people be more resilient, provide hope to others, and limit the negative impact which stressful situations can create.

People with a clear sense of purpose are more likely to emerge faster from aggravating conditions. When change is all-encompassing, it is comforting to have a goal that helps to serve as an anchor.

Now, the question is— How do we identify our purpose?

Sometimes situations are created around us, which, if leveraged well, present us with a purpose that can catapult us to great heights If we can make the most out of any situation, irrespective of limited resources, we have already fulfilled half of our purpose. For instance, COVID-19 provided a powerful opportunity for many people from medical services and other fields to find their true calling. There are countless examples of people from every walk of life who came out of COVID-19 like heroes and had a lifelong purpose.

While there will be extraordinary situations that help us build purpose in our lives, there can also be ostensibly small and "blink, and you miss it" cases, which also help us to be cautious and make the most out of everything. I recall one such incident when I was on a road trip with a batch of young trainees driving from Vijayawada to Guntur. The trainees had joined the company's Agrochemical business, and I was entrusted with bestowing them experience in the field and market.

Guntur was the country's capital of Agrochemicals, so a visit to Patnam Bazaar, the primary call for Agrochemicals, was required. Some of you may have had the chance to drive along with swaying paddy fields on both sides of roads in that area during the paddy season. You would readily appreciate the environment and mood that the drive can create. It is very soothing to the eye and the mind, and while it can lull some people to sleep, it can also send many people into a reflective, thoughtful, or refreshing mood.

So, at the end of the day, while enjoying an evening drink with the young lads, I asked them what they had observed and learned from their reflections of the day in the field and market. A statement by a young trainee, which I can recall even after so many years, still gives me goosebumps. He said that the green, swaying paddy leaves profoundly impacted him. The enormity of the opportunity to find a purpose, the scale of the canvas of what he could do, and the impact he could create in society had shaken him. What he found most energizing was the realisation that he was getting an "opportunity to be a part of an ecosystem that could help alleviate humanity's hunger problem!"

The young man Sid (Siddiqui) had his first brush with his calling, and perceived that he would be a standout leader in the years to come. From the many leaders I have observed over the years, the number of people impacted by the purpose, as well as the depth of the effect on the people, make a massive difference to the inspirational value of the purpose. Siddiqui could have had the vision to see the opportunity and then be limited by his thinking. However, like Ravi, he also started translating his vision into smaller goals and actions. Thereby, he impacted an ever-increasing circle of beneficiaries with his thoughts and actions.

Vision and action are both prerequisites for anyone to fulfil a purpose. Sometimes an opportunity presents itself to us as a recurring problem. We solve the problem and move on. A standout leader sees in that individual problem a chance to solve the same problem for so many others sustainably. Their ability to transport the individual to the collective is their potential to envision an enormous opportunity. Converting this opportunity to realism becomes their purpose.

Unfortunately, there are millions of people who have plenty of excuses regarding why they failed to achieve something. As already stated before, people find it very convenient to blame their circumstances or other people rather than take responsibility for themselves. However, a standout leader knows how to turn a problem into an advantage. A standout leader seeks opportunities even in crucial moments and fulfils their purpose. The more inspiring and loftier the goal, the more energised the leader feels for their purpose. They appear to be in a different zone, and when they talk, their words and actions have an electrifying impact on their audience. In other words, the deeper the inspiration, the more comprehensive the impact.

I have had the privilege of cherishing a good relationship with someone who has been virtually associated with the Polio Vaccination program in a leadership role from its inception. His association with the program was driven by his closest friend being a polio victim- Dave. He becomes a different person when you discuss the vaccination program with him. Everything changes, starting from his body language, tone, and demeanour, and you cannot but listen to him with awe and reverence. Dave was inspired very early in his life to see where he wanted to make a difference. His life's purpose would impact millions of lives over the future decades. He worked to create a platform that would provide him the means to give shape and sustenance to his purpose, empowered him to make decision and take actions and enabled him to live his purpose. Since the impact of his goal was wide and deep, it is no surprise that Dave is a standout leader who is widely respected.

To my readers, I am sure you have observed from the stories mentioned above that the purpose for these standout leaders helped create a much broader impact, affecting the ecosystem and society at large; their purpose also had a profound, long-lasting, and perhaps everlasting impact on people. It provided them the energy and focus to pursue that purpose throughout their lives and achieve their goals, not for themselves but for their impact on others. Conversely, if the purpose is limited and focused only on the self, immediate family, and friends, the drive and energy emanating from that purpose would also be limited. You would experience that with such a purpose, the longevity of the drive and animation also tend to be short to medium-term. Such a purpose does not drive the person through their life or career.

Most of us may find that we need a well-defined purpose which can provide us the energy and force to sustain ourselves through a significant part of our lives. There is nothing wrong with having different purposes at different stages of one's life. The focus and direction the purpose provides to an individual tends to have a shorter duration, and there could be periods in our lives where we may feel that the world is passing us by. A lot of us may find that we do not have a single purpose that defines our lives. We are often presented with situations and circumstances that require us to make certain choices. Without a clear purpose, our decision is based solely on factors that impact our future, our family and people close to us.

You may have observed that often some people reach out to the HR Department or their Supervisor seeking clarity of their job role and responsibilities. They want the roles to be precise and the KRAs well-defined. On the other hand, some people would like the functions to be a set of broad guidelines that allow for endless interpretations. A standout leader is likely to be the latter! They would prefer to be open to the role. In fact, by the time they move on to something else, they will have created a position that everyone wants to take over. The standout leader has carved out a role that did not exist earlier but has now become a highly valued one. In the process, the leader has developed himself/herself through innovation, stretching the limits/boundaries, dealing with the unknown, etc., and is now ready to test the new frontiers!

How to Identify or Articulate your Purpose?

One of the easy ways to help people identify and articulate their purpose is a two-step process:

a) List down all the activities which you enjoy engaging with.

These could include painting, music, singing, dancing, debating, writing articles, building plans & strategies, participating in areas of interest, e.g., LGBTQA+ community, watching special TV programs, reading, socialising, and so on. List down all these activities and then put them in descending order of how important they are to you and the satisfaction they give you.

One significant factor in sorting these activities would be the energy they release in you— both during and after engaging in them. These activities have an impact on you and others around you. For example, most of the disruptive changes you are witnessing today through the creation of new businesses are due to the activities entrepreneurs had engaged in for years before they came into the public eye.

Another way of identifying the areas that you enjoy engaging with and hence be able to identify the purpose, is to understand your motivators. Some of us are driven by authority, some by altruistic goals, some by acquiring expertise, some are driven by recognition, and some by creating something from scratch, etc. There are psychometric tests available that would help you identify what your key motivators are. Knowing your motivators could help you identify and articulate your purpose.

Eg. Work-life balance for some people is a key driver and they would give up lucrative and exciting opportunities if it meant compromising with the work-life balance. If they do take up roles which upset their work-life balance, they feel stressed out and eventually leave that role.

I found for myself that autonomy and freedom are extremely important to me. I used to have major issues and conflicts with a couple of my bosses who would expect me to keep them informed at each turn and take their approvals. At the same time, when I had the freedom, I could create excellent results– beyond what my supervisor would expect.

b) Draw concentric circles.

The inner one should represent yourself, the next should represent your family, subsequently friends, company, neighbourhood, community, city, taluka, district, state, country, continent, and eventually the entire humanity and the universe. These circles represent the impact you would like to have on people in different processes. The result of these circles is generated by the list of activities you have identified as the ones you enjoy being engaged with and those which energise you enormously.

The more specific you are with these activities, and the more objective you are with the depth of the impact and width of the effects that you wish to create as per the concentric circles, the easier it would be for you to identify and define the purpose of your life. It is evident that in the early stages of your life, you may find the level of impact limited to the people in the department of your organisation.

As you progress, you will find yourself stretching out to create that impact on people in the outer circles, e.g., regional teams of all departments. Suppose we were to take any of the examples or stories that have been shared earlier. In that case, we could visualise how Ravi may have started with the focus of impact on self, graduating to family, friends, an educational university, a student community, and then, a community focusing on climate at the state level.

Similarly, the things he would have found fascinating and stimulating would have been broader in his teens and youth, such as reading newspaper articles on social topics, watching TV shows, engaging in school and college discussions, and so on. Before focusing on global warming, he would have researched and educated himself on certain topics of interest. Over the years, Ravi would have continued to engage in activities that further fuelled his purpose. There is a strong likelihood that these efforts propelled him to leave an impact that is wider and goes beyond the boundaries of the state, the country, etc. The effect could be more profound and strategic in terms of longevity.

A purpose provides an overarching meaning and specifies what matters most to us. A purpose need not be fixed or static. It can evolve over the passage of time, get strengthened, build nuances and clarity. For some of us, like Ravi, it can be a lifelong aspiration– our guiding star! A purpose can attract others with similar aspirations and visions into a network. Sharing purpose with others helps us to put our stake in the ground and make ourselves accountable to the public at large. As a standout leader, our purpose can provide a beacon of hope to many who could benefit from realising our purpose. For a standout leader, a purpose provides scope, direction, degree of impact, and sustainability of bringing benefits to the community. It answers the question— "Does my existence impact anyone?"

Key reader takeaways:

- It is crucial to identify and articulate your purpose.
- Having a clear vision about your purpose *is the first step to becoming a 'Stand out leader'.*

ACTIVITY TIME!

Defining your Purpose and Essence!

Step 1: Jot down the things that excite and motivate you.

Step 2: Draw concentric circles that represent yourself, your family, subsequent friends, company, neighbourhood, community etc.

The circles represent the impact you would like to have on people occupying those circles.

The purpose starts to take shape from the several activities you have identified - the ones you enjoy being engaged with and those which energize you enormously.

To identify and define your purpose, be specific about these activities, objective about the depth of the impact and the effects that you wish to create in the concentric circles.

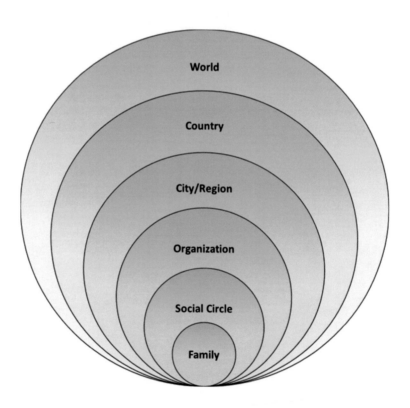

2

DISCOVER TO EMPOWER

Well, after your purpose has been defined, it is time to discover yourself completely– the strengths that you have, the weaknesses you are aware of and some that you may not be aware of which may be holding you back. It is only after authentic discovery of these strengths that can you begin to empower yourself towards your purpose as a standout leader.

At a certain point of time in my career, all the senior managers in the group companies were travelling to Jaipur. The group consisted of CEOs and the holding company's Corporate Heads, and I was one of them. It was an exciting experience for all of us as we were accompanied by two experts from the UK— Rank Xerox U.K. and PDI, a consulting company.

We were all travelling together in a bus. The purpose was to build camaraderie, teamwork and get acquainted with each other. About a year before this trip, most of the group companies existed on a stand-alone basis– each a joint venture company, with the Indian company "Modicorp" being the common shareholder. There was no connection between each of these companies except the common shareholder, Modicorp.

As a holding company, Modicorp had come into existence a little over a year ago, and the corporate structure was evolving. Hence, while we might have heard of each other, we were not adequately acquainted. Furthermore, it was essential to create common goals and interests so that a group ethos could evolve over time. Travelling for almost six hours and staying together for two consecutive days in Jaipur was a conscious decision taken to develop common bonds within the group.

Two months before the journey, we had filled out forms for ourselves and several colleagues who were our peers. We also knew that our respective team members and supervisors were filling out the forms. We were informed later it was a 360-degree assessment instrument to provide feedback on critical behavioural competencies from the Supervisor, peers and team members. We also attempted a self-assessment of those competencies. The form provided a list of questions we had to respond to on a 5 -7-point scale.

When the report was compiled based on the inputs given by the above stakeholders, we got insights on our strengths and areas of developments. Some of those were known to us, and some we discovered as our blind spots. Our first experience with an assessment questionnaire revealed what others thought about us vis-a-vis what we believed about ourselves. Moreover, as much as one should have self-confidence, one should also scrutinise their behavioural pattern for betterment.

There was a lot of positive feeling among us and a fraction of anxiety regarding what we would learn about ourselves. While there was an excitement to know our strengths, I recall that there was also a certain amount of fear that stemmed from getting to know what opinions others had formed, especially our supervisor. Most of us aboard had invested substantial time in our jobs and garnered significant awards over the years.

Each member had a good background based on performance, education, and experience in many industries. I was one of them, and I considered myself a competent professional. Back then, I had struggled enormously to identify my strengths and shortcomings. I had a hazy awareness that I loved doing and thinking things differently to popular opinion. I even thought that I knew everything and disliked losing arguments. Hence, I would investigate numerous topics to bolster my point of view.

At times, I wondered what my colleagues and team members thought of me, but these instances were few. Over the years, I have received criticism from my superiors. I have often been regarded as a good performer through my rapid progression within the organisation than by any critical evaluation. I did not perceive myself to be good at receiving feedback at that time. I seldom sought feedback. But when I did receive any input, even if ostensibly I may not show my agreement, I would reflect on it and bring around some change. On retrospection, I realised that negative feedback very seldom shattered me. My confidence was consistently high and my spirit could never be pulverised.

Hence, on that bus, there was a lingering fear of the unknown and an exhilaration of finally learning what others thought of me. The drive was exciting since several of us opted to pass the time by playing cards. I remember losing over 40,000 rupees during the trip to Jaipur and the one evening we stayed in the city— a fortune at the

33

time. I lost the maximum amount of money amongst all of us and became the butt of numerous jokes. Much later, I realised that my playing style reflected a high level of competitiveness, greater risk-taking, low impulse control, making others feel good, creating a positive environment, and taking a new approach to build excitement and not let boredom set in.

As a result, I would take risks and lose substantial amounts of money to generate excitement. Can you see how dangerous this concoction of actions is? Would I have done anything differently had I known about my idiosyncrasies? Reflecting on the incident after all these years, I am confident that I would have lost, but it would have been a fraction of what I did. Why would this have happened?

The awareness of one's conduct, mentality and thinking style aids in bringing them to one's consciousness to impact decision-making. Knowing your habits and the potential negative consequences of these activities can help you minimise your risk areas and negative qualities. However, for this to occur, a person must be conscious of their behaviour pattern. Risk-taking comes naturally to me and my reactions and responses are quick. The awareness of these behaviours helped me to ward off several problems that could have landed me in trouble. When I was not aware of my propensity for risk-taking and low impulse control, there were times when I landed into some unavoidable circumstances and had to pay a heavy price.

Have you ever been puzzled by why the reaction to your actions/conversations with others was not what you expected? Well, I discovered this the hard way! As the Head of a region, I served on the personnel committee with other regional leaders, the Business Head, and Corporate HR to assess people-related performance appraisal concerns, discipline, increments, promotions, and so on.

In two separate instances, the committee rejected the suggestions I had crafted with meticulous investigation and attention. One was eliminated because it needed to be more inventive for the organisation, and the second was postponed for six months. In both cases, my enthusiasm for the plans was palpable. My annoyance with the stated issues were evident on my face on both occasions. After all, I had invested my time and effort to develop valuable suggestions. I lost my cool and could not cogently put forth my point of view.

The Business Head took me to his room after the second meeting, and we spoke for a few minutes. From that conversation, two things remained imprinted on my mind: If something is critical and your suggestion is radical, build your support outside the meeting. Secondly, do not react negatively to objections but ride along with them, and the protests will die on their own. If they do not, the issue is legitimate and should be addressed objectively.

I realised I was coming out as a competitive person by not listening to anything and allowing my emotions to take over. For the next meeting, I spent time with the relevant stakeholders before the meeting, included their perspectives to embellish the idea and then presented it during the session. The proposal went off without a hitch! It was not 'MY' proposal anymore, but 'OUR' proposal. Earlier, my competitiveness acted as a barrier to what was best for the team. That day, I learned that working together collectively and thinking as a team instead of focusing exclusively on myself fetched better results.

Collaboration took the place of competition, and effective listening (empathy) resulted in an easy acceptance of new ideas. I will forever remain indebted to my supervisor for assisting me in acquiring these skills. I have learned a lot about myself by sitting back and reflecting on the actions that I have taken and the outcomes which I received. I found self-reflection a critical tool for gaining more knowledge about my strengths and areas of weakness.

Self-reflection is a process through which you grow your understanding of who you are, your values and why you think & act the way you do. It is a form of personal analysis that allows you to align your life with what you want it to be like. Self-reflection or introspection serves to observe and analyse oneself to grow. That growth is why it is so important to spend time in personal reflection. By understanding who you are now and who you would like to become, you help identify the steps you need to take on that journey.

When I think about the card game today, I see impetuosity,

rashness and the dire need to please people as flaws that I need to work on. I have worked hard over the years to improve these three habits of mine. While I have not been able to alter their effect significantly, I have been able to lessen their influence on my performance, relationships and so on.

Going back to the Jaipur trip, after the introductory briefing, we were given our 360-degree reports and time to skim through them and identify questions that needed to be answered. Some of us were amused by the responses of a few specific colleagues. They had argued that the wording was messed up and what they had received was not their report. Well, this is a common occurrence. Most of us go through an aspect of denial when faced with an unpleasant experience. It is usually followed by engaging with the knowledge or the situation, understanding it better, reflecting on what it means and then accepting it for what it is communicating.

Following this stage of acceptance, the next step was to respond to the circumstance or information in the most acceptable way possible. Over the years, I have observed that if the context of the feedback and information is conveyed in a non-threatening manner, individuals find it simpler and faster to transition from the period of denial to acceptance. Communication is always convenient when there is an appropriate level of cordiality.

In the given scenario, if the 360-degree evaluation had been used to identify employees with potential for advancement, it would have produced tremendous opposition to accept the information and comments. The opposition would have been generated due to the use of the information which may be inimical to my interests.

However, in this case, the purpose of the feedback was primarily to identify areas which we do well, and also areas where we were weak at and needed to put an effort to ensure that the negative impact of some of our actions were mitigated. Therefore, the movement from denial to acceptance was relatively short for some of us. Needless to say, this has been one of my most critical learnings in life.

When giving or receiving feedback, one must ensure that the

context is well understood, especially when giving or receiving developmental feedback. The inputs received during this Jaipur trip helped me move ahead in life and achieve my personal and professional goals. I learned that my strength areas were:

- ability to think strategically
- being able to identify patterns
- good ability to convince others

The developmental areas were:

- postponing decisions
- delay in execution

For the first time in my life, I was given an honest assessment of my strengths and flaws. I was never wholly unaware of them, but seeing them so clearly expressed and supported by scenarios shared by my boss and co-workers helped me comprehend my behaviours and the impact of them on others.

Have you ever noticed how others react to your unusual behaviours? Or how asking questions to understand someone else's point of view during a discussion may assist in creating a relationship of understanding and collaboration?

Understanding is not the agreement— People take a while to understand critical learning. Most importantly, I started being aware of my behaviour and actions and what effect those behaviours were having on the feelings & actions of others.

In certain situations, I would prepare myself as much as the position allowed me to. I ensured that decisions were not delayed due to my need for data/analysis and that the focus was on results rather than actions. I began using my larger-than-life thinking and influenced my strengths because I had realised I was creating more value for the company, the team and myself. My only regret is that this event occurred late in my career. Hence, the advantages could have been leveraged only over a shorter period.

If the same experience had happened relatively early in my career,

I would have leveraged it for a longer duration and helped create higher value for the organisation, the team and myself. However, over the last twenty years, comprehensive research has been done on leadership development. An extensive range of psychometric assessments are available to each one of us to help us understand our leadership capabilities and drawbacks.

Leadership and its development have been the subject of significant interest and research over the last few decades. There is barely any institution in our university that is yet to invest substantial resources of money, workforce and time in identifying how to build leadership capability. The research and leadership framework has made a profound impact not only on me but on many companies and leaders globally, especially the work done by Professor Tony Cockerill from the London Business School in partnership with organisations like GSK and the Royal Bank of Scotland. Professor Cockerill had built on the work done by other researchers & institutions, vis. Princeton, Harvard, etc.

He had created a consulting organisation called the 'Centre for High-performance Development' (CHPD) in the UK. We had the privilege of being their partners for India and built further on the work done by Professor Cockerill and CHPD by developing many leadership development processes across management levels. The High-Performance Behaviour framework identified twelve leadership behaviours that make leaders succeed in this current VUCAD i.e. Volatile, Uncertain, Complex, Ambiguous & Dynamic environment. The framework categorised these twelve behaviours in four clusters—

- thinking
- developing
- inspiring
- achieving

The details of the framework are available at the end of the chapter. The framework describes each of these leadership behaviours in simple statements and at different levels of proficiency. By reflecting on these statements, a person will be able to have a reasonable understanding of the level of proficiency they stand for each behaviour.

Young leaders can see which behaviours are their strengths and which ones could pull down their performance and ability to grab higher responsibilities successfully. Knowing one's strengths and development areas helps a person create a plan which would allow them to grow on their path of development. Research has shown that we can develop our leadership capabilities and strengths. In this book, I have shared some of my development experiences as a professional manager and situations I participated in as a professional leadership development consultant.

Most companies today have created leadership development frameworks based on the research done by various institutions, guided by their own needs and reflected through the strategy they want to pursue. Companies have recognised that leadership bench strength is an organisation's most critical asset to succeed in today's volatile and uncertain environment. Well, leadership bench strength is an organisation's ability to fill positions with a potential internal candidate with the loss of an employee.

Leadership capability expectations are not only limited to the top echelons of the organisation but are encouraged across the organisation. Most companies today have clearly defined leadership development strategies and processes as these are the vital pillars of growth and human capital. Emotional intelligence is also being recognised increasingly as a critical input for a person to be a successful leader. Research in this field over the last few decades has shown that cognitive ability alone may not suffice, and a person with high emotional intelligence is likely to succeed in today's context.

We have worked extensively in helping people develop their emotional intelligence. They used well-researched EI assessment tools like the personal emotional quotient meter (PEQM) in partnership with TMI, Denmark. We coach them on using their strengths and ways of managing/developing some limitations. A copy of a sample PEQM report is in the annexures.

I vividly recall reviewing the PEQM report of a young lady with excellent academic qualifications working for a blue-chip company in the IT sector. Her EI score was low and her profile indicated she could be heading towards depression. During the feedback conversation with her, it emerged that the young lady had just come back from a one-year stint in the blue-chip company's Paris office, which was six months after she joined the company as a fresher. One would expect a person to be in an incredibly positive frame of mind with this kind of experience and exposure in their career.

Probing further, it emerged that the young lady had taken up a computer science program against her wishes and only to please her father, a Professor of Engineering. Her career choice was not her own, but she was highly reluctant to disappoint her father, who she held in the highest regard. Very often, students pursue careers for their parents' sake and end up feeling miserable with very low self-esteem, self-confidence and a high proclivity towards a depressive mindset.

I understood her profile and how her extreme reluctance to be in the IT industry impacted her profoundly. She thanked me profusely for helping her understand her emotions and connect the same to her current role of being a Project Manager with a blue-chip IT company. There was a new resolve on her face, and newfound energy seemed to radiate. I advised the young lady to share the profile and our discussion with her father and see the outcome of the conversation. A few weeks later, I got an email from her informing me that she had resigned from her role and enrolled in a program in HRM. I could not have been happier hearing such thrilling news!

Understanding the self can create a great sense of empowerment. Many avenues are available to receive feedback on our performance, actions or inactions, attitudes and values.

We no longer need to wait for the annual appraisal cycle to get feedback (which is sometimes suited to justify the yearly rating). Many more organisations now train their managers to be particular in giving feedback to their team members. The focus of feedback should be—

- the action the person took.

- the impact the action had on that person's performance.

Hence, the feedback you get from your manager is a vital data point in completing your Leadership Capability Canvas (LCC). The feedback received from managers & other stakeholders is an ongoing process. The practice of giving feedback to each other is also more prevalent. Hence, we should be privy to receiving information about ourselves from various sources. It is now for us to take cognisance of all this information about ourselves, accept it to understand and work on it to equip ourselves better to face professional and personal challenges. An open mind is required to capture the data points.

You may follow the *Denial-Resistance-Reflection-Acceptance* route to process each data point. The positive feedback may swiftly reach the acceptance level, while the developmental or negative feedback may face more denial & resistance before reaching acceptance. In this entire sequence of processing feedback, while each step is critical, the faster you get to the reflection stage, the easier it is to facilitate some reluctant understanding.

At one stage, as a Regional Manager, I decided to take feedback from the other managers on my working style. We had a record sales month and we felt very buoyant about ourselves. I looked forward to receiving positive feedback, full of accolades, etc. In that expansive mode, I stood in front of the whiteboard with a marker to jot down whatever my team members shared. I committed to the team that I would write whatever was spoken and not challenge anything that would be stated in order to process it later. I wanted to communicate a sense of openness so that the feedback could be honest and trustworthy. What followed had me taken aback.

I was informed that I kept changing my decisions, the team found it challenging to understand the instructions clearly and I failed to share all the information required for their actions, etc. After a few comments in a similar vein, I heard someone mention that my openness to discuss issues with the team made them trust me. They believed that my decisions were objective and unbiased. I stopped writing and asked them to give me an instance where they trusted me.

I was very moved to hear this, which facilitated an openness to objectively look at the development areas and negative feedback. I requested them to provide examples for every input and I could understand how my actions impacted them. The behaviour of the big-picture thinking led to giving the road directions rather than precise instructions required at that time.

If you can create your **leadership capability canvas** *quite early in your career, there will be a higher chance for you to stand out as a leader. This profile would have many elements to it. Over the years, leaders who have been able to develop themselves always kept themselves relevant over their entire careers and succeeded at different levels. To create such attributes, one requires a profile that covers the following:*

Leadership Orientation – based on your personality and innate preference of some elements of leadership– what we call nature.

Leadership Behaviours in Practice – the way you have evolved over the passage of time.

Emotional Intelligence Profile – how do you make your emotions work for/against you?

Motivators & Drivers–what are accomplishments that mean the most to you?

Derailers – what actions could prevent you from reaching your goals?

Practiced Values – what are the core beliefs that determine your actions?

Leadership Capability Canvas

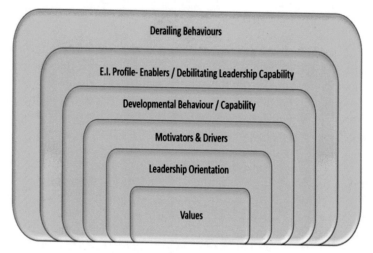

Copyright Inspireone consultants Pvt ltd.

Make your Leadership Capability Canvas a dynamic instrument for change.

You would keep receiving inputs from various sources– people, family, bosses, other stakeholders and various assessment tools during your career. Keep recording your LCC and note how you are evolving as a person and leader.

In my second year as a student at the Faculty of Management Studies (FMS), University of Delhi, I was elected the General Secretary of the Management Science Association. It was a unique honour as I had never occupied any position of such responsibility in my school or under-graduation days. I was elated and felt I would leave behind strong footprints as a General Secretary. In the past, the General Secretaries would carry out routine activities of organising matches, picnics, interdepartmental and interfaculty students' matches, etc. However, I wanted to make a difference.

In the previous year, IIM Calcutta had organised an inter-institution convention with participants from IIM Ahmedabad, XLRI Jamshedpur, Jamnalal FMS Bajaj Mumbai and FMS Delhi. In the competitive environment of the institutions, this was a big feather in the cap of IIM Calcutta. Taking a cue from them, I decided and sold the idea to other office bearers of the MSA that we should hold a similar convention at FMS Delhi.

A concern arose around resources as the University refused to support us financially. As students, we took up the challenge and organised resources from the industry, which was not an easy option considering the time when everything was not readily available like it is today. We got great support from some of the industrial units and lined up some great speakers for the convention.

All the major Management institutions came to the convention. It was the first-ever convention at a student level organised at the FMS. At the Convention, Professor Subramaniam Swamy, (at that time he was a Professor with Indian Institute of Technology, Delhi)) enthralled the audience with his banter and ability to paint the bigger picture. I remember being applauded by the then Dean, Professor Abad Ahmed, who introduced me to the then Vice-Chancellor of the University, Professor Swaroop Singh, with great affection and pride. In the same year, we took a team of over fifty students on an educational trip to the various industry units in Mumbai and a recreation trip to Goa.

We managed to get a grant from the University Grants Commission for this educational & industry exposure trip, and the students had to pay a minimal amount. We organised a bogey from the Indian Railways, and it was probably one of the best experiences that the students had as a part of their education over the years. I made my mark as I had originally planned.

Similarly, other situations come to mind when a burning passion to be different and a great need to leave a mark was the leitmotif for my actions. Very early in my corporate career, I identified that doing things routinely was not my cup of tea. So, if I were to say what motivates me, how it describes me and what my essence is, it would probably be greenfield, entrepreneurial and unique actions. I discovered that authoritarian behaviour in others brought forth the hidden rebel in me. What is it, dear reader, that you can identify for yourself as the core you? Your reflections on situations where you have achieved significant successes would help you discover your passion, motivators & drivers!

Jot down the significant achievements that you have had in your career so far, including the student phase. Identify what it was that motivated you to achieve what you did. Is there a common thread that you can see across all these achievements? (Check out the annexures on Drivers). It is essential to be aware of these. Without this knowledge, you may spend significant time performing actions that do not necessarily motivate you. You could be investing a considerable effort in an area to which you aspire, but for which the core motivators still need to be added!

Discover Your Mojo!

Everyone is not obligated to aspire for a leadership role. Being in a leadership role and displaying leadership behaviours are two different things. A person could be in a leadership role and not display leadership behaviours resulting in massive stress for the incumbent and a significant loss of value for all the stakeholders- `team members, the organisation and the person himself.

At the same time, a person may be in an individual contributor role and yet display significant leadership behaviours of strategic thinking, building great inter personal relationships, being able to network extensively, take challenges, being innovative etc. Whatever be the role a person may be performing it is important to understand your key leadership strengths as well as your limitations.

It is fundamental to understand that while your strengths work for you, the improper use of force could be your biggest derailer-your biggest weakness. It is like a batsman on the cricket field who has the best square cut in the game and has scored maximum runs square of the wicket with that stroke. However, most dismissals of such batsmen have also been in the square or 'point' region.

It is a fact that your strength can also be your biggest weakness. A colleague of mine was recognised by all of us (his friends) as being very competitive. This competitive behaviour permeated all his actions and hindered his collaboration and working with others as a team. It also led to his habit of not sharing information and becoming secretive.

Consequently, he became aloof and felt ostracised. His ability to work collaboratively with teams went downhill. His career plateaued quite early as he needed help managing the transition from being competitive to somewhat less competitive and more collaborative. In situations where individual performances were more critical than team performances, the competitiveness of this colleague would have fetched him better rewards. However, his extreme competitiveness became a millstone around his neck in the corporate world, where you must be more collaborative.

Being competitive is not negative behaviour. If competitiveness is used positively, it will shape you differently. But drowning too much into the rat race of competition can majorly scar you beyond repair. When one's behaviour becomes obsessive, the negative impact has the potential to destroy both personal and corporate values. There are enough examples of family businesses/wealth going down the drain due to extreme competitiveness amongst the family members.

It is crucial to understand your strengths and how, if they are very intense, you should guard against their overuse. If these strengths become obsessive, their impact turns from being positive to negative. You should tone down that skewed strength so it does not start destroying value for you. These strengths can turn out to be your derailers. Can you identify your derailers?

The leadership capability canvas helps you plot your values, motivators, drivers, derailers, displayed leadership behaviours, leadership orientation, and so on. Your inputs could be from the feedback you received from various sources, more structured inputs from assessments, and most importantly, through your self-reflection sessions.

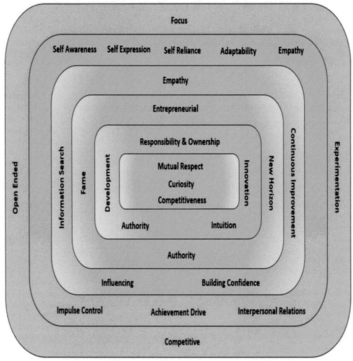

Sample Leadership Capability Canvas

The green colour indicates a positive impact on leadership capability. The orange indicates derailers & emotional intelligence factors that could limit an individual's leadership capability. Too much competitiveness, lack of focus, and achievement drive can hinder an individual's ability to strive.

Key reader takeaways:

- Self-discovery and awareness are critical success factors to be a 'standout leader'.
- It is crucial to identify your drawbacks along with your

strengths. It is also important to identify strengths that may be derailers when overused.

ACTIVITY TIME!

Discover and Create an Empowering Personal Development Plan:

There is only one process available to achieve the metamorphosis of a leader to a standout leader, self-development. The starting point of self-development is to know where you stand today.

The process of SELF-DISCOVERY!!

Once you have identified your leadership strengths & gaps in the various parameters, what do you do next?

A standout leader would always be on the path of development and refinement. I would strongly encourage all young leaders to create a Personal Development Plan based on:

- My personal & professional goals over the next 3-5 years

_____

_____

_____

_____

_____

_____

- What leadership capabilities would I need to achieve these goals?

_____

_____

_____

_____

_____

_____

- What leadership capabilities do I possess based on the Leadership Capability Canvas?

_____

_____

_____

_____

_____

_____

Development Plan

Here are some questions to use when you are coaching yourself or someone else on creating a personal/individual development plan. Rephrase them so they work for you and add your ideas.

Creating a Personal Development

- Plan Checklist
- Facilitation questions

Objective

- • What would you like to learn/achieve?
- How does that link with your business objectives? Why is that business objective important?
- What could you do to make your job easier?
- What is that one thing which would improve your performance?
- What is the present situation? How would you like the situation to be different?
- What is stopping you from achieving your goals now?
- On a scale **of 1-10, where are you now overall in your career?**

Action Steps

- How do you learn best? (Tailor action steps to suit Learning Style)
- What will you do to get there? What comes first? When will you do that? How often?
- With whom? In what situations?
- If action means to 'get feedback', then what is it about? In what situations? From whom? How will you get it? When?
- What could you do to change the situation? What alternative approaches are there?

Support & Resources

- What support do you need? How and when will you get that support?
- Who might be able to help? How?
- What resources might you need? Where could you get them?

Success Criteria

- What results will you be achieving?
- How will you know you have reached your goal/s? What will you see, hear and feel?
- What will others notice? What feedback will you seek?
- On a scale of 1-10, where will you be (vis a vis your long-term

goal) when you achieve your objective?

Timelines & Review

- When will you achieve your objective? How will you measure how you are doing?
- What systems will you put in place to monitor progress? What milestones are there on the way to achieving your objective?
- When & what will you review progress to ensure your success criteria?

Goals

- Is the goal SMART?– Specific, Measurable, Attainable, Realistic, Timebound?
- Is the goal challenging? – e.g., is the scope of the IDP goal larger than your KRAs? Is the IDP target number higher than the KRAs?
- Is the target date mentioned in the day-month-year format? What is the underlying reason for you to work on this action plan? What will achieving the goal mean to you?
- What new thing/skill/behaviour are you learning/building on by the end of this goal?
- How will the goal impact your business KRAs? How will the organisation benefit from you working on this IDP?
- How will this goal contribute to your overall career progression?
- Who else do you know has achieved something like this? How did they do it? What can you learn from them?

Measures

- Is the success measure linked to the goal?
- Is the target measurable? [E.g., 'increased trust in the team' is not a quantifiable target. However, a score of 8 on the trust meter is a measurable goal.]
- Is there an indirect measure you can use? Who will review the success measure?
- Are your success measures linked to your KRAs? (If not, consider modifying them.)

- What are the in-process measures you will use to review your IDP progress?
- What are the specific targets used to measure the success of the project? Is there enough stretch built into the targets? How will you know how far you are from achieving your goal? If you had a new manager and needed to convince them of your achievement year-to-date, what would you use as a yardstick?

Action Plans

- Is the action linked to the goal?
- Will these actions get you from the current to the desired state vis-a-vis the goals and the target competencies? Define your critical path.
- Is the action measurable?
- Are there too many action steps defined? Can any of the actions be clubbed together?
- Can any of the actions be further divided to make them measurable? Will the omission of any of the action steps affect the overall goal? (Check this for each action statement and remove the unnecessary actions)
- Do your actions use the tools/techniques you may have learned/read about?
- What will get you to achieve your goal?
- Is there another way to achieve the same goal?
- What resources do you have that you need to use? (i.e., skills, time, support)
- What might be a risk and its mitigation?
- Training– is it possible to complete these activities on time? Is the institution organising these training programs or will they be self-led?

Competency/Behaviour

- Have you selected one strength and two development areas to work on?
- Are these behaviours observable and measurable?
- Are the behaviours selected for development critical to your role?

- Are the behaviours selected for development critical to your goal? Will movement on the desired behaviour contribute to action on your overall goal?
- Is this part of a more extensive behaviour? Can this be broken down further to make the impact of the behaviour measurable?
- Is the selected behaviour overlapping with a KRA?
- What has been holding you back from showing movement in your development areas till now? How can you combat those factors now?
- How did you identify your target behaviours?
- What is the desired level to be sought for each target behaviour?

Overall

- What will you need to do before and after you start working on this IDP?
- How will you ensure that this process is on track?
- How will you track your progress– how often will you review yourself?
- How will you document key learning from the process?
- What are the possible roadblocks? How can you circumvent these?
- Who are the stakeholders you need to involve? How will you keep them engaged? Who else can you apply to if they do not show interest in your IDP?
- Is there anyone you know who is working on a similar project? How can you collaborate with them?
- Have you considered working with a learning buddy?

THE HIGH PERFORMANCE BEHAVIOUR FRAMEWORK

THINKING CLUSTER	
RATING	**GATHERING INTELLIGENCE**
5	Sets up strategies to build a rich information environment in the unit or wider organisation. E.g., by systems to gather and distribute information, surveys, or a regular programme of information gathering visits. Builds a value for the systematic collection and use of information.
4	Searches a broad range of information from other parts of the organisation or the external environment. E.g., information about new technological developments or relevant economic, political, social and demographic trends or the practices of comparable organisations or competitors.
3	Searches broadly across the major categories of information relevant to the specific task, problem or issue being considered. Searches sufficient categories of information to arrive at a comprehensive understanding of the specific task, problem, or issue being managed.
2	Narrow information search, misses important categories of relevant information about the specific task, problem or issue. Search limited to questions of clarification of information given or being presented.
1	Uses pre-existing assumptions as a substitute for information search; no information search; denies, rejects, distorts or closes mind to information.
RATING	**GENERATING IDEAS**
5	Sets up methods or processes in the organisation to encourage others to form broad, new concepts. These concepts may explain trends, events, issues and processes occurring in the organisation as it interacts with its environment. Or the concepts may be new visions, options or solutions for the future.
4	Links information relevant to a specific task or issue with information from the wider organisation and/or the external environment to form powerful diagnostic concepts, visions, options or solutions. E.g., sees graduate wastage and customer dissatisfaction as both being caused by a hierarchical structure with too many levels that is unsuited to the organisation's fast moving, competitive environment
3	Forms diagnostic concepts, visions, options, or solutions that are bounded by the specific task or issue being managed. The ideas formed do not integrate wider organisational or environmental information with the specific issue or task being managed. E.g., sees the remuneration package for graduates as the cause of their high wastage rates.
2	Does not form new concepts; uses existing concepts or concepts provided by others. Links categorises or classifies information but does not form new concepts. May exhibit difficulty in understanding the concepts used by others.
1	Inhibits or prevents the development of new concepts by stating implementation problems or by citing past experience; lowers the level of the concept being used. Uses pre-existing concepts not anchored in relevant data.

RATING	ACCELERATING INNOVATION
5	Sets up processes or encourages others to create several different, diagnostic concepts to understand what is happening and to generate multiple visions, options or strategies whose pros and cons are compared before action is taken. Builds a value for the use of conceptual flexibility in the unit or organisation.
4	Compares the merits of two or more realistic alternatives, by stating the pros and cons of each. May create an over-arching plan or strategy as a result of this analysis that maximises the benefits and minimises the downsides of the original options.
3	Uses at least two alternate diagnostic concepts to understand what is happening in the unit or environment. States the different concepts or perspectives held by other individuals or groups. Develops at least two different plans, strategies, or options. The alternatives must be viable, approximately equal in value and held simultaneously.
2	Can see different diagnostic concepts, perspectives or options but does so at different times. Does not hold these concepts, perspectives, or options simultaneously i.e. serial rather than parallel processing of alternatives.
1	Adopts a single plan or strategy. Rejects alternatives that are relevant or valued by others. No evidence of the perception of alternative concepts, perspectives, or options.

DEVELOPING CLUSTER	
RATING	ESTABLISHING TRUST
5	Develops strategies or processes that encourage people (customers, staff, suppliers, and other stakeholders) to fully and openly state their true ideas, feelings and beliefs. Builds a climate of trust and openness in which people are valued for saying what they really think, feel, and believe and can do so without any fear of criticism, judgement or punishment.
4	Tests and validates own understanding of another's ideas, feelings, or beliefs by using paraphrasing and summary clarification to ensure that their perspective or viewpoint is fully understood. Discloses own true ideas, feelings, and beliefs to enable others to do the same.
3	Uses open ended and elaborate questions to find out the ideas, feelings, and beliefs of others. The aim is to see issues, events, ideas, explanations, or options "through the eyes of another" - to really understand their mind- set. Is non- evaluative and non-judgmental in understanding the perspectives and viewpoint of others.
2	Listens to others carefully, shows recognition of the value of others' contributions.
1	Closes down opportunities for others to express their concepts and ideas; e.g., through interruptions, evaluations, and over- concern for the presentation of own views. Interrogates others to build up a case against them; uses questioning following the statement of own views to exert pressure to conform to that view.

RATING	FOSTERING COLLABORATION
5	Builds strategies and processes to encourage open team interaction and team development. Creates strategies for cross-boundary teamworking e.g., between different functions, business units, geographical areas or organisations. Creates a climate which values team interaction to build shared team concepts and strategies that go far beyond the initial ideas of the team members, and which break down the conceptual barriers created by territorialism and turf warfare.
4	Facilitates dialogue between two or more team members so they create shared "team concepts" that are more powerful than any of the individual ideas that were contributed at first. Ensures that the dialogue continues until a comprehensive set of team concepts has been created.
3	Facilitates dialogue between two or more team members so they come to understand the linkages, connections, patterns or similarities between their ideas or options. Ensures that all team members understand the linkages being made. Brings team members into the dialogue to ensure their contribution is fully realized.
2	Does not engage in managing the interaction. Shows interest in the interaction; does not disrupt or close down interaction.
1	Behaves in ways to shut down the contributions of others, e.g., centralises interaction around self; persists with own expressions regardless of what team members are doing; imposes a false or premature consensus on the group; makes unilateral decisions. May also prevent interaction between individuals, teams, and units by having them report in individually, meeting with them separately and discouraging lateral communication.

RATING	DEVELOPING TALENT
5	Sets up strategies to build a supportive and develop- mental environment that enhances the capabilities of people and enables them to realise their potential. Creates ways for others to coach, mentor, train, recognise and give constructive performance feedback to others. Systematically provides others with challenging responsibilities to foster their development. E.g., by a programme of secondments or lateral transfers to other functions, businesses, or countries or by the creation of a network of mentoring/coaching relationships.
4	Takes personal responsibility for supporting and developing others by acting as a mentor, coach, or trainer. This involves modelling effective behaviour, getting others to practice this behaviour and using constructive feedback to enhance their capabilities. Allocates important projects and challenging responsibilities to another for the purpose of his/her development.
3	Uses training or development courses or programmes to enhance the knowledge or skills of others. Recognise the achievements of others and the actions they have taken to develop themselves. Supports others' efforts to develop themselves.
2	Makes general statements about the need or value for training and development but does not translate this into actions.
1	Shows no concern for development when the need exists; fails to support others' developmental efforts or to give performance feedback. Reduces or restricts the responsibilities of others so that the developmental nature of their work is lowered. Holds the view that others are unable or unwilling to learn or develop. Creates a climate in which under-performance or mistakes result in threats or punishment.

INSPIRING CLUSTER	
RATING	**INFLUENCING PEOPLE**
5	Builds strategies of win-win alliances between own and other teams, units or organisations to gain mutually advantageous resources and goals. Creates a climate which values and uses socialised rather than unilateral power i.e., shared interests rather than domination, persuasion rather than imposition, win-win rather than win-lose or lose-lose.
4	Forms win-win alliances with others by showing how the realisation of own interests or goals will support their interests and goals which therefore justifies joint planning and/or action. Uses this approach to build political support for needed change or resources for own team, unit or organisation.
3	Attempts to persuade others showing the specific advantages, benefits or features of own ideas, plans, strategies, products or services.
2	Presents own position without any attempt to persuade others to buy-in. May expect own position to be so persuasive that it is not necessary to try to influence others to buy-in.
1	Attacks others' interests or positions and is consistently negative toward their ideas, in an attempt to promote own interests. May attempt to force others down own preferred route through coercion or by using threats.
RATING	**BUILDING CONFIDENCE**
5	Creates processes or methods to boost the confidence of internal or external stakeholders (e.g., staff, customers, owners, and suppliers) in the present and future success of own team, unit or organisation or in their own capacity to succeed. E.g., sets up regular events to enable participants to share their successes and build excitement, confidence, optimism and hope in the future.
4	Personally builds the confidence of others in their own capacity to succeed or in the future success of their team, unit or organisation. Makes statements to build hope, optimism, excitement and enthusiasm in others. Demonstrates own belief in and high expectations for the success of a particular plan or strategy.
3	Makes timely decisions in a self-assured way when demanded and confidently justifies and maintains own position or decision when challenged. Is resolute in the face of criticism or setbacks. Demonstrates confidence by facing up to and tackling difficult or delicate issues. Lets others know own stance or position. States and justifies a necessary change in direction in a confident manner.
2	Avoids taking decisions when required. May continue searching information when a decision is needed. Shows hesitation or doubt when justifying own position. Changes mind without justification when challenged. Shows ambivalence about stating own stance or position thus leaving others unclear or uncertain. Avoids difficult, delicate or controversial issues.
1	Creates a climate of pessimism, doom, despondency and doubt about the future. Expresses own lack of belief and confidence in the success of the team, unit or organisation. Creates confusion and uncertainty by consistently changing decisions, own stance or position or by systematically avoiding difficult issues.

RATING	COMMUNICATING EFFECTIVELY
5	Builds communication strategies to present clearly and concisely the team, unit or organisation to internal or external stakeholders. This ensures stakeholders are well informed and have up-to-date information about the purpose, strategies, performance, needs etc., of the team, unit or organisation. Builds a value for outstanding presentations and encourages others to stress the need for excellence in communication.
4	Commands the attention and interest of the audience by the use of technology, visual aids, gestures, voice modulation, humour, analogies, compelling content and momentum. The core message is projected vividly and with vitality.
3	Presentations and other verbal communications are clear, concise and well-structured with good eye contact and minimal distractions. Key ideas are communicated with economy and clarity.
2	Presentations are understood but are impaired by factors such as limited eye contact, low volume, high speed, distracting movements or the poor structuring and expression of ideas and content.
1	Presentations are difficult or impossible to understand due to factors such as inadequate eye contact, very low volume, very high speed, ineffective movements or because the expression of ideas and content is characterized by extreme verbosity, repetition or rambling.

ACHIEVING CLUSTER	
RATING	IMPLEMENTING CHANGE
5	Sets strategies to get others to take actions to change the internal or external environment so it provides greater opportunities and more freedom of action for the team, unit or organisation. Creates a climate that values and encourages people to take the initiative, to remove unnecessary bureaucratic constraints and to broaden the scope of their responsibility to ensure necessary action is taken. Encourages others to become the masters of their own destiny.
4	Reduces the internal or external constraints on self and others to enhance the freedom for action and the scope for initiative. E.g., redefines the boundaries of a market or industry; redesigns jobs to allocate more responsibility to the people closest to the customer; strips away unnecessary bureaucracy.
3	Designs implementation plans including the actions to be taken, their sequences or phases, and responsibilities or roles for self and others involved in the implementation process.
2	Is responsive to the plans and initiative of others. Takes action but in a reactive way to the ideas of others or environmental events.
1	Does not take or resists taking action because it would violate existing norms, rules procedures, directives or the traditional way of doing things. Shuns responsibility for anything that falls outside the scope of own existing responsibilities. Narrowly defines the scope of own responsibility to restrict own range of action. Cites the actions of others or external events as the cause for own shortcomings.

RATING	IMPROVING PERFORMANCE
5	Envisions or establishes a strategy to develop and perpetuate a balanced scorecard of specific, measurable targets. These targets must span the major dimensions of team or organisational performance (e.g. financial, customer, people development and organisational development).
4	Establishes an interconnected set of specific, measurable targets designed to raise at least two, different, dimensions of team or organisational performance.
3	Sets a specific measurable target designed to raise some aspect of team or organisational performance (e.g. customer satisfaction or process efficiency or cash flow or profitability).
2	Verbalises general statements about the need to improve performance but sets no specific measurable targets.
1	Sets targets that have no reference to incremental performance improvement, being content to leave things as they are. Denies the ability to set performance improvement targets or resists others' attempts to do so. Uses performance standards as a means of controlling and/or punishing others.

RATING	WINNING CUSTOMERS
5	Builds a strategy to fundamentally raise the importance of customers in the team or organisation. The strategy must contain an integrated set of initiatives which establish or redesign visions, business processes, organisation structures, reward systems etc. so greater value is added to customers.
4	Takes an initiative (a clearly interconnected set of activities) designed to raise the value added to customers. These activities will have a wider or longer-term effect than a specific action designed to address a particular customer issue or problem.
3	Takes a 1-off, specific action to raise value-added to customers by meet-ing a specific customer request/solving an immediate customer problem. The action addresses the immediate issue but has no wider effect.
2	Makes general statements about the importance, value of customers, but no specific actions are taken or planned. No evidence of a concern for adding value to customers.
1	Accepts or reinforces an inward-looking approach that is not focused on customers. Does not respond positively to requests or feedback from customers. Resists or undermines actions of others designed to add greater value to customers.

3

LIFE IS A LAB

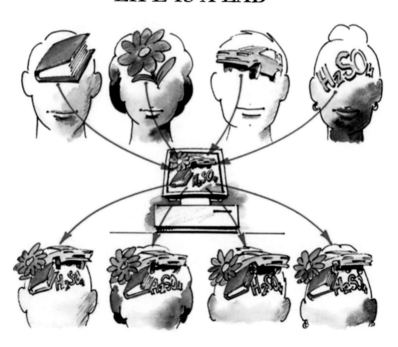

After creating an **empowered development plan based on self-discovery**, *it is imperative that this development should happen on-the-job. Development efforts cannot be divorced from the actual work you do. They must be embedded in and result from your role and goals. Therefore, life – work and personal - is your lab.*

One fine morning, I received a letter from the Director of Business Operations stating quite unambiguously that the performance of my business unit was at acritical level, and in the Xerox world, it would require significant intervention. I had been in Modi Xerox and this job for over six months, and to get such a letter from my immediate supervisor was quite unnerving. I recall that the letter was triggered by a complaint from one of the office supplies dealers. The dealer complained of the delays in getting the consignment and the damaged condition in which the consignment was received. Moreover, this had become a regular feature and caused damage to our brand.

Modi Xerox was going through a global initiative called 'leadership through quality' with a strong focus on customer & process improvements through the total quality management approach. I had also received training as a part of this initiative and thought of putting my learning to practice. I wanted to see how I could improve the business unit's performance in the areas mentioned. I formed a team of five members from different functions, including finance, marketing, logistics, IT and myself. Over the next eight months, we focused on:

- understanding the customer's requirements
- identifying various aspects of the problems
- brainstorming possible solutions
- implementing the most practical solution
- evaluating the results & modifying the solution
- finalising the process
- rolling it out across the country

While brainstorming possible solutions, a novel idea emerged of using clearing and forwarding agents and setting up the processes at their end. This was a light asset-based solution and quick to put to trial and evaluation. C&F agents and services already existed and did not require the company to invest in new infrastructure. The option to buy the services vs build the infrastructure to provide these services was clearly in favour of buy. The critical requirement as setting up the processes, training the C&F agency staff, defining clear deliverables, and putting the Service Level Agreements (SLAs) in place for delivering as per customer commitment.

We engaged on an experimental basis for six months at one C&F agency, evaluated the results against all parameters, and got the results validated by our internal audit team before launching it across the country over the next two years in a phased approach. The initiative was a resounding success and helped improve customer scores and the business unit's overall financial performance.

When it happened, as a part of the global initiative of leadership through quality, Modi Xerox organised country-wise competitive events where teams were encouraged to present their projects for improving processes in line with customer needs (customer being internal or external). Our team also decided to participate and we put in our project as one of the entries for the competitive event. It was one of the most fulfilling moments of my professional life when our team won the President's Gold Medal for 'The Best Project' in India.

The impact of this initiative and the overall experience profoundly affected my behaviours and actions after that. My process of thinking became more structured and process driven. No longer was it a conscious effort to jot down steps for problem-solving or process development. Unconsciously, the mind would seek information, process the inputs and quickly evaluate the idea's feasibility. The clarity of thinking that evolved thereon was an excellent capability that developed from that experience and became sharper with time. Furthermore, a compelling set of questions got developed which helped in resolving many issues over time:

- Who is the customer for the output that I am producing?
- What is it that my customer wants?

These questions remove a lot of clutter from the mind when you are jostling with too many ideas/information/problems, etc. The clarity of 'who is my customer?' and 'what are my customer's requirements?' have proved to be the proverbial compass that has helped to successfully wade through many challenging situations and problems. If one were to reflect on the actions taken, one could clearly see healthy behaviours emerging of:

- customer focus
- continuous improvement
- result orientation
- innovative thinking
- collaboration

(Please review the behaviours vis a vis the High-Performance Behaviour table for better understanding.)

It is vital to understand that working on even one real-life project can help a person create fundamental changes in his leadership behaviours that it will have a sustainable impact on all future performances. Over time, consciously using these actions can help build an unconscious competence and capability. These are crucial leadership behaviours triggered by a supervisor's feedback on unacceptable performance. The acceptance of feedback itself reflects an excellent ability to focus on self-development. When we reject feedback, we deny the opportunity to make ourselves a better leader. Hence, it is imperative to accept constructive feedback gracefully to enhance our skills. 'A Complaint is a Gift' is a book written by a good friend Janelle Barlowe, for the Service Industry, which is relevant for self-development.

Development Model

The 70-20-10 model for learning and development is a widely accepted norm to describe the optimal sources & methodologies of understanding by successful managers. Development happens 70% from job experiences, 20% from interactions and feedback with others, and 10% from formal structured learning situations. The 70-20-10 model is a general guideline that organisations seek to maximise the effectiveness of their learning and follow development strategies.

The model suggests that the job experience has the maximum impact on a person's learning as it enables them to explore, experiment and learn from their successes and failures. In the process, they can make decisions, seek information from within & outside the system and interact with relevant stakeholders such as bosses, customers, and competitors. Employees learn from others (20%) through various activities that include social learning, supervisory feedback, structured review sessions, coaching, mentoring, industry forums, collaborative learning and other methods of interaction with peers.

Lastly, 10% of professional development comes from formal learning events like training programs, workshops or other events that impart profound knowledge. These percentages vary depending on the learning objectives. The above percentages are a good guideline for leadership development. The story of Modi Xerox shared above is a prime example *where 'on-the-job-learning' worked optimally for the team as the 70% mentioned in the model.*

This is the reason this chapter is christened with the title – LIFE IS A LAB!

One can learn a lot from reflecting on actions that assist us in achieving what we did, as well as reflecting on actions that came in the way of achieving our goals. The opportunity that is enumerated above is an example that has been discussed previously. You can give many situations where you may have succeeded or even failed. One of the most critical and successful ways of developing leadership capability is to work on projects that challenge an individual's competencies and capabilities. If most situations we encounter during our professional or personal life do not challenge us, then the scope for development as an individual is significantly diminished.

In my experience, if you want to develop someone, give them a tough project to deliver. In most cases, it is likely that one of the supervisor's critical projects can be delegated to the team member for his development. In the process of working on that project, the person will have to exhibit actions and behaviours that would make it possible for the project to be completed smoothly.

If you want to develop someone in Sales, and the development needed is strategic thinking, then it is unlikely the person would develop these capabilities of information search, idea generation and innovative thinking by picking up a project on a marginal increase in sales by10or 20%. Instead, asking him to develop a market coverage plan for a new territory would help him look for different aspects of customer definition, customer needs, competitive strategies, logistics and many other factors to develop an innovative market coverage plan. In the process, the person would start developing behaviours of customer focus, information search and others which is the development need of that person. Of course, some element of coaching is undoubtedly required from the supervisor to support this.

This story was shared with me by a colleague who was the Marketing Manager of an Agrochemical company. We were discussing the development of team members, and he referred to this event during his tenure as a Marketing Manager. A young Area Sales Manager got transferred to his team as a Product Manager for his most promising product portfolio. The young Product Manager had no prior experience in a similar role. Still, he had done exceptionally well as an Area Sales Manager in one of the Eastern states, wherein he showed great imagination in building a business virtually from scratch. Not only was he imaginative and very result-focused, but also, he had the zeal to thrive in his field. His role as a Product Manager would help him build capabilities of long-term planning, creative thinking, critical problem solving, and influencing. These qualities were crucial for leaders who were expected to grow in the company's former critical roles.

My friend, Kapadia, the Marketing Manager, shared how the new Product Manager, Vivek, needed clarification on the role for the first few months. Kapadia felt it would be a good idea to ask Vivek to develop a long-term marketing plan, virtually a business plan, for the most critical product of the company for the next five years. Kapadia would have generally taken on this responsibility as he was required to present this plan to the division board and, eventually, the company board.

The product was critical in the sense that it contributed to over 50% of the company's revenues and accounted for over 70% of the company's gross-contribution. Kapadia met with Vivek and explained the assignment's criticality and that of the project he was handing over to him. He asked Vivek if he would be keen to take the role. Vivek, of course, was exhilarated to be given this mission-critical project. His enthusiasm weighed heavily on Kapadia's mind when he entrusted this project to Vivek. Kapadia felt that Vivek was reasonably familiar with the overall business as he had been in the company for over three years, worked in the field, understood customers and their needs, and was aware of the competition.

However, Vivek's knowledge was limited to a part of the market rather than the entire market, and it focused only on sales & not the overall business model. Kapadia advised Vivek that he had three months within which the project needed to be completed and would be available to Vivek when required. Kapadia realised that Vivek was very independent in his thinking and appreciated a high degree of autonomy when he requested that he would give him an update once a month. Hence, Kapadia should not expect a weekly update and work status. Against his better judgment, Kapadia agreed to this request even though it was a mission-critical project for him too. However, he did not wish to demotivate Vivek and agreed to delegate the entire assignment to him.

As it turned out, two weeks later, Kapadia was down with jaundice. His recovery was slow, and he found himself away from work for almost seven consecutive weeks. He spent less time at work and the project receded to the backburner both in his memory and in immediate criticality. The Director of the Business Unit understood the situation and agreed with Kapadia that the product's Long-Range Plan (LRP) could be taken up a couple of months later.

Three weeks after Kapadia rejoined and almost three months after handing over the LRP project to Vivek, Kapadia was pleasantly surprised and somewhat taken aback when Vivek handed over a glossy, well-packaged & well-documented report entitled LRP. While going through the report, Kapadia was amazed at the quality of thinking, creativity, problem-solving and eye-to-detail that the report communicated.

On discussing with Vivek how he had approached the assignment, Kapadia was delighted to hear the entire story. It was a well-known fact in the industry that more than 70% of that specific class of agrochemicals were consumed primarily by one crop—cotton. Hence, any long-range plan would require a deep focus and understanding of that crop. Vivek relied heavily on the data which was published in a five-year study conducted by the National Council of Applied Economic Research (NCAER) on Agriculture in India, including cropping patterns, the area under various crops in different states, the quality of seeds, the quality of produce, the incidence of pests and so on.

It was evident that the cropping area of cotton fluctuated every year based on the prices of the crop in the preceding year. Thus, Vivek had to create a database of cotton prices over the last few years to understand the correlation between the costs and the cotton acreage in the following year. He also had to see the irrigation plans for the next ten years to understand the growth in cotton acreage. In addition, he had to understand the usage of cotton and how that would change in the coming years. The usage of cotton was again dependent on population growth, the use of cotton in textiles, especially in mixed fabrics with cotton and synthetics and the use of cotton in areas other than clothing, exports, etc.

As it is obvious from the above, the variables were countless, and Vivek had to focus on a few vital ones which had a significant bearing on the growth of cotton acreage, the quality of the cotton crop and the quality of cotton fibre. Different quality of cotton fibre is dependent on various factors various qualities of seeds; soil conditions, weather conditions, and so on. Another set of variables was the incidence of pest attacks on the cotton crop and the farmers' practices of spraying the agrochemicals on the crop, both quantity and frequency.

The farmers' practices were also not consistent across all regions and states where cotton was grown but varied from region to region depending on temperatures, monsoon conditions, soil conditions, etc. Vivek studied all these factors and developed a multiple correlation and regression model, which you could then extrapolate for the product's usage pattern over the next five years.

During the three months, he worked with his colleagues in different regions and encouraged them to share their knowledge of the farmers' practices. He looked at available secondary data and travelled to a few states to get first-hand information from the farmers he could interview. He immediately made a series of fixed assumptions, which he constantly validated from the Area Managers and Visual Managers so that he would have a higher buy-in from the field organisation.

Sharing this detailed story with me, Kapadia was overwhelmed remembering the kind of effort that Vivek had put in to create a world-class report which had no problem sailing through the board and making a huge buy-in with the entire sales organization. Based on that report, the company decided to expand the capacity, even though the capacity utilisation at the time of writing the information was less than 50%. Kapadia shared that the company was able to overwhelm the competition with its aggressive approach to product and availability and that they were the unquestionable market leaders in the upcoming years.

As a leader, Kapadia felt extremely vindicated by his decision to empower Vivek to create the report and grant him the independence and autonomy he desired. On the other hand, Vivek showed extreme information search behaviours, generating ideas, innovative thinking, self-confidence, ability to influence others and result orientation. During this initiative, Vivek developed himself as a leader with strong capabilities in the above-mentioned leadership competencies. These capabilities cannot be developed purely through workshops or structured learning alone. These capabilities can be honed and mastered only through working and applying the knowledge in an actual situation in the real world.

In the end, bookish knowledge does not cater to dealing with the real world. Your self-confidence, presence of mind and skills help you survive. You see the impact of those actions on your performance, and that reinforces if what you are doing is correct, and you make it a part of your regular repertoire. It was not surprising that Vivek became a Regional Leader well ahead of the typical career plan and became the youngest & successful Business Leader with another company.

To be a standout leader is to be someone who picks up challenges and learns from performing well despite those challenges. In managing the challenges, the person builds an armoury of leadership capabilities. The capabilities for addressing those challenges stand the person in good stead in the future. Of course, the sustainability of these capabilities requires a strong dose of self-reflection. While developing the plan, Vivek did not glance at the first option that presented itself. He kept on challenging himself to travel beyond the obvious and realised the diverse relationships he needed to examine to devise an optimum solution. In a way, he innovated a possible option from many different options he could create.

Secondly, he took the actions, identified patterns, evaluated the output, and reworked what was different from his expectations. For example, while looking for information, he did not simply accept what was available within the organisation, but went out in the field to the competitors, noticed primary data, looked at the research available, and then identified what could be the drivers to the consumption of the agrochemicals on cotton. Without performing actions, it becomes difficult to evaluate your strategy.

Finally, Vivek would not have been able to achieve what he did had he had not taken a few risks— the risk of taking ownership and accountability, the risk of exploring different approaches, the risk of making projections that were way beyond anyone's imagination, and finally, the risk of carrying everyone along with the approach. In the entire process, Vivek took inputs from different stakeholders within and outside the organisation, shared his assumptions and received feedback with openness from others.

All of the above factors indicate a high degree of learning agility, which is critical in today's fast-changing world. In the book of Living Life, adaptability and adaptiveness to new emerging situations are the most critical facilities expected of today's leaders. To be adaptable and to adapt to conditions requires a powerful ability to keep learning consistently and continuously.

Adaptability is the ability to deal with a changing situation where the future appears uncertain, information on what is impacting the future is unknown or scantily available, and there may need to be more capacity available to deal with fast-changing scenarios. An exciting story helped me understand the difference between 'adapting' wherein the situation overpowers you and you veer away from your long-term goals, and 'adaptability', where you take steps & modify your actions to achieve your long-term goals.

I met a friend after many years, and we exchanged notes on what had happened in the last five-six years since we had last met. Rahul, my friend, was an IIT-IIM alumnus and had an impressive academic background to make a mark as a standout leader. He started his career with a blue-chip company and over the next few years, moved on and joined a growing new business as a Sales' Manager. During the conversation, I learned that he was looking for a job and had been without one for the last few months. Intending to understand and see how I could help him, I asked how the present situation had come to pass.

The last company with which he had worked for over ten years had closed because their product had become obsolete. With a sense of pride, he told me that he did not let the team down and stuck it out till the end and was one of the last few people to exit. During the process, he had accepted salary cuts, appreciating that the business was not doing well. Rahul felt he kept on adapting to the situation right till the end. On further probing, he revealed that the company failed to realise the advent of new substitutes and how they could slowly take away the entire business!

It was quite evident that Rahul and the other leadership team members were caught napping and did not know how to manage in the fast-changing business environment. Rahul should have shown the leadership behaviour of 'adaptability' by sensing the changes brewing in the industry and responding proactively to the fast-changing environment. He felt adaptability was accepting the situation and going down with the ship. Unfortunately, the lack of critical leadership behaviour in a wonderful profile like Rahul brought him not much success. Had he realised this earlier, he would not have been a victim of the situation.

Learning Agility – (Innovating, Performing, Reflecting, Risking)

Modern challenges require modern ways of addressing them. It is essential to ask yourself this question – Is there another way of looking at the problem? To keep learning, one must constantly look for new challenges, which requires the whole cycle of innovation, performance, reflection, and risk-taking. Research has shown a high degree of correlation between emotional intelligence and learning agility. Hence, it is good to understand and leverage that to build a strong learning agility capability.

Another aspect is of reflecting on the various actions like:

- What steps did I take?
- Why did I take that action?
- What was the impact of that action on the people, output, and consequential responses?
- Was the effect that what I wanted?
- What other measures could I have taken?
- What were my feelings while taking that action & after taking that action?
- What can I do to sustain positive actions?

These reflections enable you to bring consciousness to the actions which you may have taken somewhat subconsciously. It helps you to determine the raison d'être of the actions and allows you to chart out a new course of action than the one your subconscious mind is accustomed to. In this way, you will be able to comprehend the path you chose for working in a certain way to achieve specific goals and how this could become a way of life for you, both cognitively and emotionally.

Key reader takeaways:

- Most of our development can and should happen on-the-job.
- It is, therefore, important that from on-the-job performance you:

o Reflect,
o glean, and
o analyse successes and challenges, to identify which behaviours worked and which need to be developed.

Life, after all, is a lab. The tools given below will help you to leverage life as a lab.

ACTIVITY TIME!

The exercises given in the next few pages will help you in build your ability to reflect.

CREATE YOUR OWN VISION:

This exercise will help you establish and focus on your aspirations.

Imagine a date 5 years from now - imagine your ideal life at that time.	
Imagine five years from now what an ideal typical day would look like.	
What would you be doing in work life and personal life?	
Who would be around you?	
What would be your thoughts and feelings?	

BUILDING POSITIVITY

Allocate time to spend on things and people you enjoy.

Things you enjoy doing	Your action Plan: When will you do this? How will you do this?	When will you review this?

People you enjoy being with	What activities can you schedule with people you enjoy

MANAGING STRESS

Be aware of what happens physically and mentally when you feel stressed. Identify your stress triggers & signals.	
Identify your stress management techniques.	

How will you apply the factors stated above & whose help will you need?	

Additional resources:

You can access these free Stress Indicators to determine your current stress levels:
http://www.hse.gov.uk/stress/standards/pdfs/indicatortool.pdf
http://www.stress.org.uk/stresstest.aspx
http://faculty.weber.edu/molpin/healthclasses/1110/bookchapters/selfassessmentchapter.htm

MANAGING NEGATIVE THOUGHT PATTERNS & DISTORTIONS

Review your thought processes and identify negative thought patterns. Link to Cognitive Distortions.

Cognitive distortions are not rational. They can instigate thought processes that lead to destructive behaviour. How often do you find yourself using these distortions? Rate yourself from 1 to 5 with 1 being low and 5 being high in the table below. Choose one of them and monitor your thoughts and correct yourself when you get caught in distorted thinking.

Score (1-5)	Thought Processes
	1. 'All' or 'None' mindset: You see things in black and white categories. If you fall short of perfect, you see yourself as total failures.
	2. Over generalisation: You see a single negative event as a never-ending pattern of defeat. Phrases like "You always" or "You never"

	exemplify over generalisations.
	3. Mental filter: You pick out a single negative detail and obsess on it so that your vision of all reality becomes darkened, like the drop of ink that discolours an entire glass of water.
	4. Disqualifying the positive: You reject positive experiences by insisting they "don't count" for some reason or other. In this way you can maintain a negative belief that is contradicted by your daily experiences.
	5. Jumping to conclusions: You make a negative interpretation even when there are no definite facts that convincingly support your conclusions - a 'wait and see attitude' is called for in these situations. **Mind reading:** You arbitrarily conclude (usually by personalizing their behaviour) that someone is reacting negatively to you, and you do not bother to check this out. **The fortune teller error:** You anticipate that things will turn out badly, and you feel convinced that your prediction is an already established fact.
	6. Magnification (catastrophising) or Minimisation: You exaggerate the importance of things (such as achievements or someone else's goof up), or you inappropriately shrink things until they become tiny.
	7. Reasoning: You allow your negative emotions to colour how you see the world with an "I feel it,

	therefore, it might be true."
	8. Statements: You try to motivate yourself or others with should and should not, as if you are being punished. Should statements often bring out anger.
	9. Personalisation: You see yourself as the cause of negative external events which in fact you were not responsible for.
	10. Labelling and Mislabelling: Instead of describing your error, you attach a negative label to yourself, "I am a loser." When somebody else's behaviour puts you off you attach a label, "He is a jerk." Mislabelling involves describing an event in language that is emotionally loaded and not truly descriptive.

4

LIFE IS A LAB: LEADERSHIP TRANSITION

Once you start to leverage "Life as a Lab" for your personal development as a leader, it is time to expand the lab to development and transition as a leader.

During the course of my career as a professional and a consultant, I have come across various definitions of a leader. A definition that really resonated with me was — 'A leader is someone who helps others achieve their potential and even beyond that.'

In other words, without the leader's presence, a person would have been unable to achieve what they could have done or what they did with the support of the leader. This definition resonates with me because the focus is on adding value to your team members rather than yourself. Imagine a team of five members reporting to you. How can you add value to each one of them? As a team leader, have you ever asked yourself this question? Most of us focus on the achievement of our own goals rather than supporting & ensuring the fulfilment of the goals of every individual in the team.

Probably, the most significant change a person goes through in his personal life is when a person becomes a parent. Vital changes occur overnight in your lifestyle, leaving you overwhelmed, and you have no choice but to be a willing partner in that transition. Over the next few decades, you feel a sense of responsibility for your child's development, academic performance, extracurricular activities, and so on.

Does anyone feel unhappy about making that transition? NO!

Do we rejoice when our children shine in several fields over the years? YES!

We take pride in the performance of our children, even when they are mid-career, and never shy away from sharing their promotions/increments/media coverage with our friends, etc. We celebrate their growth and bask in their glory. We feel elated by their victory. Similarly, in the professional world, when we assume the role of a leader, we take ownership of how the individuals in our team performs in their roles and future careers.

Some of the proudest moments in our careers are when we learn how a person who had worked with us progressed in life and emerged as a standout leader. You share with the entire world instances of their past, when they were a part of your team, how you were always aware of the spark in them, how you helped them to grow, how you helped them make choices at critical times, etc.

How do we take actions today so that we can create the above scenarios in the future? What steps can we, as standout leaders, take today to help us recount stories of future standout leaders that we helped to develop? For this to happen, the big transition you must go through is from managing yourself to managing a team and people. The making of a standout leader starts with this transition! So, how can a team leader help develop standout leaders of tomorrow? What are some of the critical actions & strategies standout leaders put into motion to inspire the development & creation of more standout leaders?

Developing People

In most organisations, during the performance appraisal process of a leader/manager, there is an absence of parameters that focus on the question, 'How many team members have you developed during the course of the year and in which areas?'

I urge every leader, and especially the young leaders who are very competitive and focused on their involvement, to understand that our growth cannot happen without you focusing on the growth of your team members. In other words, you must be aware of your members' strengths and development needs, and have a clear plan in your mind of how you will help each person in your team.

I want to recount a minor incident that helped me appreciate how focusing on the development of one's team members can create significant trust between the team leader & the team members. We were running a development centre for a multinational Pharma & Consumer product company. They had invited their senior members, not only from India, but also from different parts of the globe. The development centre was conducted in India and the participants included people from Brazil, Japan, and Portugal.

After the development centre was completed, we encouraged the client organisation to organise a tripartite discussion between the participant, his supervisor, and the HR department. The objective of the tripartite discussion was for the participant to share with their supervisor what they had discovered during the development centre process and the areas they would like to focus on for their development. The supervisor was expected to actively listen to what the participant had to share and formulate a development plan for the next couple of years. The presence of the HR was critical to ensure that the plan would be incorporated into the company.

It was an excellent process, but I was still determining to what extent this company would go to for all the participants. I had a few participants from India who were easy to organize logistically. However, I had one participant, Soares, who was the CFO for the company's Japanese operations, reporting to Japan's CEO and country head. Logistically, it was challenging to organise because the HR head of the APAC region was based out of Australia, the CEO of the Japan unit was traveling, and I was based out of India. However, the HR Head ensured that the tripartite virtual conference did take place, and for that one hour of discussion, the focus was entirely on the participant i.e., Soares.

Now, I want you to visualise and put yourself in Soares' shoes. How would you have felt when there was so much attention being focussed by everyone on your development? Soares was at the centre of everyone's consciousness for that particular hour, and the entire team tried to help him identify his development goals. I found this to be exhilarating and have recounted this incident several times to help senior leaders understand and appreciate how the investment of their time in developing their team members is of utmost criticality.

This is the mark of a true leader; this is the mark of a standout leader. No wonder the company that I am referring to is a global leader in the Pharma & Consumer product industry and is widely known for its progressive people policies. Another story which I am always bold in recounting is that of a life insurance company in the private sector, which was languishing at the bottom of the competition at that time. A new CEO and CHRO had taken over recently and decided to invest in developing a few high-performing individuals as a strategic initiative to build capability and improve the company's performance.

The CEO had also decided to invest in individual coaching for all the CXOs to ensure an alignment with the new strategy and focus on some critical behaviours that would be relevant for successfully implementing the process. The whole initiative lasted for over twelve months. During the given period, I had the opportunity to meet the CEO and CHRO on various occasions. I was highly inspired by the CEO's focus and hawk-eye on the progress.

I remember vividly when all the thirty-three participants shared their progress over the year, including the change in their development areas, the CEO sat through two days of presentations and closely followed the successes, challenges, failures, and improvements in their own behaviour. It was not surprising that when the CEO invested so much time and effort in the development of people, it became the entire organisation's sole mission over time. In a matter of three years, this life insurance company had taken over the number one spot in the private sector among other private companies. Not only this, even the CEO went on to lead one of the largest private-sector banks in the country and ran it successfully.

Leaders across sectors and industries realise that people development must be an area of core focus and personal interest to them if they must leave a legacy of institution-building behind them. Working only for your own betterment shall bear no fruit in the longer run. A standout leader must ensure that people development is a strategic focus for every leader. As a team leader, you must know each team member's strengths & weaknesses, especially concerning their roles.

Delegating development to other professionals/coaches/ trainers is a common way that most leaders follow. But investing your time in the development of your team members and taking personal responsibility for their development is the hallmark of a standout leader. The CEO of the Private Life Insurance company took personal responsibility, just like the CEO of the Multinational Pharma Company, demonstrating exactly this point.

In your opinion, what is a stronger message of a leader's focus on people development— sending a few people every year to one of the most prestigious development programs or personally coaching and mentoring a couple of people from his team or organisation every year? I am keen to know your views and the thinking behind them. A leader may adopt any strategy for developing his team members and is free to do so within the constraints of the company's resources and priorities.

However, what could be more impactful is the leader's commitment to the development of each of his team members. A leader is a standout leader by virtue of how many leaders he developed & created during his lifetime. Many senior leaders have articulated that they do not have any KPIs for developing their team members. If a leader is going to act based on KPIs alone, then it is likely that they would never be a standout leader. A leader has to lead people and help them achieve what they cannot by themselves.

Empowering People

Another incident that hugely impacted me as a young leader was a town hall meeting called by the CEO of Modi Xerox. It had been barely a year since I had joined the company. The company's performance was extremely below its plans for the year. Dr. BK Modi, the CEO of Modi Xerox at the time, had called this town hall and requested all the team leaders to identify one or two projects they would like to undertake. He specifically advised them to keep their thinking within a sufficient amount of resources. Forty-five team leaders were assembled at the town hall, and I was one of them. Each leader was given five to seven minutes to present their case, provide an idea of the resources they required and give up a page to the CEO's office.

We were all quite hopeful that the resources would be sanctioned and we could implement our ideas. Each of us had worked with our teams before the town hall had gone through the process of generating ideas. There was a certain degree of trepidation that our ideas may be ridiculed, the resources would not be made available as per our requirement, and eventually the whole exercise may become frivolous.

At the end of the town hall, after listening patiently to all the ideas, Dr. Modi approved them along with the resources and advised the finance department to organise the resources for implementing those ideas. He also set up a date 30 days later for a review of the projects or the implementation of the ideas. Within a span of six months, the company had turned around, and the resource utilisation was only 30% of what had been asked for.

Tell me, what do you think had happened? What miracles did the teams do to achieve what they did? Why was their resource utilisation so low compared to their demand? At that time, I did not dwell so much on these questions. However, after reflecting on this a few months later with some colleagues, we realised that what Dr. Modi did was:

- empowered us
- helped us clear our self-imposed constraints
- helped us remove our internal inhibitions & cleared our cobwebs
- created tremendous confidence and self-belief in each one of us
- built a powerful display of his total commitment, support and belief in us.

Most of the time, our self-belief, or lack thereof, is the biggest enemy in achieving our potential. A good standout leader helps the team to build that belief and confidence to say, "Yes, we can!" President Barack Obama had given his clarion call, "Yes, we can!" during his first presidential elections, but I must confess that I had witnessed this many years before. Leaders deploy various approaches to develop their team members and help them achieve goals that may be difficult for them to attain on their own. I have come across some of the approaches as stated:

- sharing a big vision and helping team members be a part of that vision.
- challenging the team members to believe in themselves and extend their boundaries.
- empowering them by leaving them to their own devices & learning along the way.
- coaching them through complex projects and helping them succeed.
- helping a team member achieve their first success and supporting them through it to ignite self-belief and self-confidence.
- closely monitoring and supporting them through complex projects.
- ensuring the availability of critical resources which may not be

so readily available to the person.

Can you think of some?

Leading Disruptive Change

I was two months into my role as General Manager of a new business unit in Modi Xerox. I had joined MX after leaving my earlier role, where I was the Head of Sales of the largest business in that company. When I joined Modi Xerox, my mandate was to set up a new division for selling large equipment. The typical sales cycle after my joining was between eighteen to twenty-four months, and in the last five years, the company was able to sell just two units.

I went through a vast period of dissonance with regret for letting go of my previous job. Suddenly, from being the most important person in the company, I had become an inconsequential employee in a new company. One afternoon, while I was in a state of misery, I realised I had a meeting in a few minutes with Dr. Ramsbottom, a Consultant from Rank Xerox UK. Dr. Ramsbottom used to visit India quarterly, meet with key critical managers and some of the new members of the leadership team to get their perspective on how the business ran and what could have been done better.

I vented the immense disappointment and regret stored in me for leaving my previous company. Dr. Ramsbottom heard me out patiently for an hour and replied carefully, "Deepak, I shall be back in three months. At that time, I may not find you here or you would have sorted out your problem successfully." After he left, I ruminated on what he said. My first instinct was to return to my previous role, which I knew was available. I also knew that the management would be more than delighted to have me back. Another part of me revolted against this idea of going back. Accepting defeat without making any efforts to make a success of the undertaking I had taken up would be pointless. I wanted to challenge the discomfort that was mounting within me.

Over the next few weeks, while I tried to establish the business for which I was hired, I constantly reflected on what I could do to make myself significant to the new company, as I had been to my previous company. I realised that my ego had been somewhat bruised. I wanted to gain the same importance I had earned at my previous workplace. However, I was determined to use this challenge to create something for which I would be remembered and respected. When I reflect on this today, I realise that my reactions of being valuable to an organisation I was involved with were consistent with my behaviour in the past– in institutions where I had studied (FMS) and worked (Rallis) or organisations I had been engaged with (ASSOCHAM). I had an ardent desire to feel important and leave an ever-lasting impact on people.

An idea emerged in my mind over the next few months. At that time, Modi Xerox was globally run on a business model whereby the photocopier machines were sold directly to the end-user and customer. So, the salesforce was humongous and forever growing to meet the needs of market coverage and customer requirements. It has been a successful model in every country for decades. Over the years, my strength has developed in channel distribution.

On the other hand, the strength and strategy of Xerox were focused on direct sales. In my mind, I was convinced that a direct sales model needed to be more sustainable for a country as varied and extensive as India. We would develop a third-party distribution channel to effectively cover different customer segments and markets across the country.

The direct sales business model was reasonably effective in dealing with government and large corporate accounts. However, this model is less cost-efficient in dealing with other smaller customer segments. To reach the different customer segments of mid-size businesses, we require a more cost-effective model of reaching out to them. I was convinced that it would be easy to persuade others. However, I also realised that the current direct sales strategy was heavily ingrained and impossible to challenge and change.

If I were to bring around a change in the distribution strategy, then an ally would be required strategically. I knew if I broached the idea with any of the people from the operation, who were committed to the current system, they would kill the idea even before it was allowed to germinate in anyone's mind. I was new to the company and needed to build my credibility within the system. At the same time, I had a very high conviction in the idea and was extremely passionate about taking it forward.

After a great deal of thought, I wrote a short concept note on the benefits of having a third-party distribution channel, an Indirect Channel (IDC) to address the emerging market segments of small & medium-sized businesses and how India, being a nascent market would be the best location for an experiment in the Xerox world. I sent this note to my Director, who was on a three-year assignment to India from RX, Europe.

I was delighted to get a call from his office suggesting a meeting with him the next day. I had an extraordinary meeting with him and I realised that he was keen to do something unique and innovative during his tenure in India, which posterity could remember him for. The Indirect Channel (IDC) idea appealed to him, but he was not ready to provide the leadership and sponsorship yet.

The Director suggested that I discuss the idea with Dr. B.K. Modi, the MD & President of the company. If he sponsored the idea, Xerox would be open to it. I met with Dr. Modi, who immediately loved the idea and asked me to create a project plan and collect the resources required to make it happen. I received the green signal to implement my theory and, hopefully, a new business model for Xerox! Over the next two years, I worked on the IDC project and brought a dream to a business reality. By the end of the two years, which also coincided with me leaving Modi Xerox to return to my previous company as the Business Head, we had created a viable new INDIRECT CHANNEL virtually in the Xerox World!

I felt good leaving behind a legacy:

- A vibrant team that was managing the business and growing it.
- A growing network of over 15 channel partners created
- with a dedicated team for the MX Business with financial resources and a passionate owner who believed in the future of the business.

and management processes were documented and people were trained.

experience dealing with an IDC system. Thus, both the functional skills and the skills of managing a Channel partner, who is not an employee or team member, were required to be ingrained in the DNA of the team. Remember, this occurred in an organisation where the norm was direct selling. Okay, so tell me, how do you create a space for a team where all the support systems are not aligned with your business model?

For example, the dealer account reconciliation process was to be managed by the Accounts team. This was not a priority for them as they were preoccupied with existing direct sales & business issues. In any case, the contribution of the IDC business was a minuscule 2% of the total revenue. So, what could be the possible solution? – Get a dedicated Accounts person to support your business by selling the idea as an investment for future business growth and not as revenue expenditure.

I started this story with a situation in which I was pondering the possibility of leaving my new job with all its limitations and returning to my previous job. I conclude that story by recounting what eventually became one of the biggest successes of my career. In the process, I built up an armoury of leadership capabilities that I could leverage in the future.

The project helped me to discover, stretch and develop my potential. If I had not taken the challenge of pushing for a disruptive change in a successfully running business model, I would not have learnt all that I did. The change from an existing successful strategy is the most challenging goal to aim for.

So, what problems are we trying to fix with the proposed change? Several objections can derail you from your passion, but does that mean one should not focus on achieving complicated goals where disruptive change is the only option? Should we think about change only when we are in the reactive mode, that is, when change is the only solution to survive?

The following framework helps elucidate the dilemma of 'when to change' most eloquently. This model is based on the theory of 'The Life Cycle Curve,' which is relevant to all human beings, including individuals, companies, governments, nations, and empires. However, unlike human beings, organisations are not biologically limited. If companies are wise, they can jump onto new curves once their first cycle shows signs of decline.

The problem is that most managers need to be made aware of this decline as a tool, heed the warning system and make the necessary adjustments in strategy before it is too late. The frequent culprit in business failures is the time gap between when an organisation's focus, energy and enthusiasm decrease, and when the results are inevitably noted in their financial balance sheets. If the best time to change is during period A (as shown in the figure below), most companies do not realise this need for change until late in period B when energies are low and resources have been sapped.

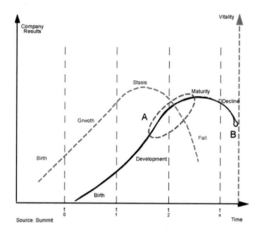

This curve reflects the company's overall level of energy and, in this case, intersects the Life Cycle Curve in the A area. How do you identify whether the organisation/team has the vitality of Period A or Period B or any other Period on the curve between A & B? The best solution is to keep a close track of enterprise vitality based on a Vitality curve— the broken line. A simple way of gauging the vitality of your team is to identify what you believe are the critical 5-6 factors that reflect how committed they are to their roles, goals, and team outcomes. Some of these could include the following:

- level of participation in team meetings
- number of new ideas generated
- responsiveness and timelines being met
- collaboration between team members
- how many BFFs are within the team
- clarity on team goals
- problem-solving as a team

Plot a score for each member on the selected parameters every week, and see how the barometer changes. This becomes your 'Team Energy Meter', guiding your decisions on bringing in disruptive change. A sample' Team Energy Meter' is given in the annexures. Kindly refer to it. A leader becomes a standout leader by sometimes creating disruptive changes, setting challenging goals, taking stands and defending difficult decisions. The inability to defend your choices will weaken your resolve in the longer run. To take tough decisions does not mean being inflexible in your approach, even when information suggests that your decision could be wrong or someone else has a better option to yours.

Building Trust

Building trust

What is that one factor which can negate or be the antithesis of being a standout leader? Unequivocally, based on my experience, a person in a leadership role focusing on the 'self' rather than the 'team' cannot be a standout leader. A few years ago, I went through a book on trust and discovered a fascinating factor called the trust equation. Based on empirical research, the trust equation postulates the direct association of faith with relationship, reliability & capability and an inverse relationship with self-orientation.

While relationships, capability and reliability directly affect trust, self-orientation probably has the maximum impact in destroying trust. To be a standout leader, you must ask yourself a vital question whenever you take a critical decision- Will the benefit of this action or decision accrue for the team, a team member or myself? If the benefit is for yourself, then it is a case of self-orientation. That decision will clearly not help you become a standout leader but in fact, will destroy the trust you could have created with positive actions in the other three areas of relationships, capability and reliability.

As a young Regional Manager, I was once faced with a difficult situation. One of my team members, R. M. Chopra, an Area Manager, had been doing consistently well for the last eighteen months despite difficult business circumstances. In all the quarterly reviews, he received very positive feedback for his initiative.

Undoubtedly, I saw him as a person who was ready to take over my role in the next twelve months. In my mind, I was convinced that he should be recommended for an upgrade and identified for development to the next role. In this connection, I had discussions with my supervisor on a couple of occasions, and he indicated that he would favourably consider him at the appropriate time.

After the annual appraisal, I gave my inputs to my supervisor for all the Area Managers in my team. I reflected upon the performance of the particular Area Manager, whom I strongly recommended for promotion. I was taken aback when their increments and promotions were announced, and my recommendation for the concerned person was discarded. I sought a meeting with my General Manager and shared why I felt my recommendation was ready to upgrade to the next level.

He listened to me patiently and said he would talk to the HR again, but he was still determining if any effort would be fruitful. However, he promised me that he would consider it for next year. There was no strong rationale for why this promotion could not be given despite an outstanding performance. When nothing happened for a week, I felt compelled to write a message to my General Manager with a copy to the Director again, emphasising why I thought that this promotion was critical for the interest of the company and the team.

While writing the letter, I was concerned about my own future as I was rocking the boat by taking an adverse position. A couple of days later, my director called me for a meeting, heard me out and commended me for persisting with recommending a case which he also agreed with. As an exceptional case, R.M Chopra was promoted. The problem had been that his promotion was coming within two years of his last promotion. However, my rationale and his own performance helped us secure a promotion that had been denied to him earlier. I felt vindicated. But most importantly, I felt satisfied that I had taken up cudgels for a team member's interest and not my own. There was no self-interest involved at all.

What do you believe was the impact of this on R.M Chopra? It is crucial as a leader to project your high performers to the forefront. This would raise your esteem and their trust in you. If you believe in what is correct, you must pursue it to its logical conclusion, especially if it involves the interest of others. You are likely to face obstructions and objections, but you must find ways to manage these challenges.

Conviction in what is right and self-belief will help you achieve goals that may seem impossible at times. Understanding the implications of the other three factors are also necessary— relationship, capability and reliability. As a young leader, it is vital to spend time outside office with your team members individually and collectively. The relationships created outside the office environment help us manage the formal relationships within the organisation precincts.

During our school and college days, most of us had built friendships that lasted for decades. Similarly, relationships and friendships at the workplace have an excellent opportunity to forge a powerful bond of kinship. I have seen many marriages between two young people from the same organisation get solemnised. I have even witnessed deep relationships between colleagues getting forged and continuing over the years. A senior colleague and a close friend of several years, Prakash Nanani, is my benchmark of a person who built trust based on forging intense relationships with his team members. Prakash retired as the Managing Director of Xerox India a few years ago. He invested his time and emotions in building relationships with people at all levels and not necessarily at senior levels alone, which some of us sometimes do.

With his ability to build relationships, Prakash was able to generate a degree of trust with most of his colleagues. Even in situations where he had to make decisions that may not have been in favour of the individual, the concerned employee would never doubt Prakash and realise that things were beyond their control. The trust was implicit and the sense of fair play was taken for granted. Well, of course, this trust was primarily built on the personal relationships that Prakash could generate with each individual. He genuinely appreciated being at the same level as his colleagues. Even with sales people, he would be very humble and eat at roadside eateries (dhabas) with as much relish as the next person. He never let his position and ego create a wall between his colleagues and himself. He defended his team members a lot, so they would never be afraid of taking actions that had risks. Furthermore, he was open to vigorously promoting the cases of his team members for critical career postings and development programs.

Inviting people home with their spouses helped him deepen the relationships from the individual to the family level. More than anything, investing his time with colleagues in areas other than work helped him build bonds, which were strong even decades later. He developed this strength further by consciously channelising his instincts into two leadership behaviours of empathy & interpersonal relations. These two leadership behaviours helped him earn the trust of his team & colleagues.

You might have been asked sometimes- who is your 3 a.m. friend? In this question lies one critical behaviour of reliability. It is assumed that this person would leave everything for you when you need them. One person who most people would vouch for being their staunchest supporter would be their mother. It is instinctive that this one person would reach out to you no matter what the circumstances might be. Do you have a person in your professional ecosystem who is in the same reliability circle as your mother? Someone who would be available when the need arises? If you are such a person to your team members, you are already on your way to being a great leader.

At the beginning of my career, I was posted as an Area Manager in Orissa, and I had a Regional Manager, S.B. Roy, based in Kolkata as my Supervisor. I was only a few months out of B-school and reckless enough to believe I would conquer all alone. As it happened, I was assigned to start a new sales office in Bhubaneswar, Orissa primarily because it was a start-up operation with negligible business, managed largely out of Kolkata. The potential was not expected to be significant, and it was a low-risk, small operation where a youngster, fresh out of B-school, was not expected to do much damage.

In any case, the eastern region did not contribute and Orissa was the smallest within that pile. Mr. S.B Roy belonged to a time when authority was never questioned. He had been in that role for over two decades and was reluctant to move to Mumbai for more senior positions as he was content to be the lord of the eastern fiefdom. A relatively new Director of the business, K S Anantharaman (KSA), was a role model to all of us. He was pleasant, encouraging and a great listener. He would make time for us even when he was invariably elbow-deep in work. He was at one end of the spectrum of leadership, where S.B Roy was on the other end.

From day one, my Regional Manager tried to control me and I avoided him. I did not want instructions on what to do daily. I wanted to think for myself and then take action. Luckily for me, the regulatory conditions for the fertiliser movement changed and our operations in Orissa suddenly got escalated from 500 MT /pa to over 15000 MT/pa. One fine day, I was suddenly in the spotlight. My Regional Manager, HQ management and my Director were interested in getting regular updates. From being a risk-free operation, it became a high-risk operation, according to my Regional Manager. The level of interaction or interference further increased.

Within a short span of time, I found myself hiring sales

associates, appointing dealers, meeting government officials, finalising contracts with the cooperative society, etc. I was as busy as a bee and kept traveling in the summer heat when the mercury was touching over 45 degrees Celsius regularly. What was more troubling for me was the regular nit-picking being done by the RHQ team from Kolkata. I was constantly under a barrage of questions about delays with no offer of any support. During that period, my director used to speak to me every week, encouraging and motivating me, offering suggestions, and never ridiculing my thoughts, even though some of them were preposterous, which I realised later.

However, the situation between Kolkata and me was heating up and regular letters were being exchanged, the language of which became sharper every day. The business was doing well, but there were some aspects where I needed improvement. Suddenly one day, I heard that KSA and S.B Roy were coming to Bhubaneswar to review and meet some government officials. So, the Regional Manager directed us to schedule the meetings with the Agriculture Commissioner and the Secretary. I was a year into my job and less than eighteen months out of B-school. The RHQ believed that I would fail the test.

My director spoke to me about the visit and advised me on how to organise his meetings with the government officials, etc. The conversation was so nurturing that my fears ebbed out of my system and were replaced with energy and positivity. My gut feeling told me– my director had my back! I put all that I had into organizing the meetings with the senior government officials. I became acquainted with the Agriculture Secretary by being a member of the same IAS Club. I met with him at the club and sought his time for a meeting with the bosses.

In turn, he urged me to get a company membership in the Corporate Club. The visit was a resounding success, and KSA projected me within the RHQ and the government as one of the company's most valuable employees. At that very moment, I knew that I had a boss who was reliable, encouraging and protective of me. For me, he was as reliable as my mother, but in a professional context. He was my leader not for his position or role but for building my confidence.

The Journey so far, for becoming the Standout Leader:

As a young leader, with an eagerness to stand out in the pantheon of leaders, I have found the following four critical leadership capabilities:

- Developing your team members
- Energising & inspiring your team
- Creating growth through disruptive change
- Fostering trust

In the previous chapters, we discussed the following:

- The need to have a purpose– a deep-rooted core that empowers and drives your actions.
- The critical aspect of understanding your leadership strengths and development needs is through various psychometric tools and the process of reflection.
- How to create your development plan and work on your leadership capability development while on the job by tackling stretch projects and challenging myself.
- How to develop yourself further as a standout leader by creating strong enabling conditions for others to perform beyond their potential & emerge as leaders.

Key reader takeaways:

- It is vital for a leader to be aware of the strengths and weaknesses of their team members.
- It is critical to challenge your team members to work towards their potential, above and beyond the expected performance.
- Develop and empower team members. Celebrate successes.
- Leading disrupting change can be challenging but one must think strategically instead of giving up.
- It is mandatory to build trust among team members in order to work together, create cohesive momentum and achieve beyond what is expected as a team.

in the IT organisation.

Furthermore, the Account Manager is also responsible for erating revenue for the company. The Account Manager sees ir role and contribution at a more value-adding level and can netimes adopt a superior tone & tenor when talking and mmunicating with the project team and the Project Manager. Over e, they may inevitably start shielding access to the client for the ject team. In turn, the Project Manager views the communication m the Accounts team & Account Manager as a directive, ronising, talking down and so on. With limited direct access to client, the project team's dependence on the Account Manager m becomes even greater.

Moreover, the Project Manager sees the Account Manager as a lleague at the same level and accordingly views the relationship as tween two equals. They cannot understand and accept that the count Manager should relate to them in the manner that they do. ver time, this builds up resentment and sooner than later, it results a clash of ego & thereby conflict. As a result of this ego clash & nflict, project timelines get pushed, quality issues start developing d customer satisfaction takes a nosedive. If the situation persists, e company may develop a dissatisfied client.

As you can visualise from the above scenario, the customer's nterest and requirements differ from the goal for which the two takeholders are now working. There must be a misalignment

5

ACT: ALIGNING, COLLABORATING & TEAMING

So far in the book, we have discussed the development of a standout leader through

articulating a clear purpose, having self-belief and developing one's leadership capability through our experiences in the cradle of life's lab. We have also elaborated on how from being a team leader, we can become a standout leader by ensuring the growth of the team members through capability development, energizing & inspiring, building trust through empathy & setting disruptive forces into play to jump the growth curve.

The next significant step to being a standout leader needs new boundaries and rules of the game to be created in order to be ahead of the race. For this to happen, you need to break the confines of the team & even the organisation in your pursuit of leaving a mark. In fact, most leaders find this transition and movement away from the comfort of their team to be a significant challenge. The careers of most managers tend to hit a speed-breaker when they try to move beyond a team leader's role and be a leader to all other leaders. Why does this happen?

Having studied and consulted with many organisations, I believe that to jump the curve from team leader to leader of a leader, there are two critical capabilities needed:

- Aligning, collaborating and teaming
- Influencing and creating networks

Both capabilities require a person to be away from his team and spend time with people & groups outside his circle of control. Most team leaders loathe being in a situation where they have limited to nil authority and yet must achieve results that can only be done by creating joint interests. Creating a common interest requires someone to shed some of their personal interests. Leaders believe that with their authority, they can command their claim to be protected. Two leaders having similar views of the world and equal keenness to protect their respective interests are unlikely to develop a solution that could be acceptable to both.

Leaders get so used to wielding authority within their team to achieve goals that they cannot use any other capability except authority to achieve them as this requires efforts and consent from others who do not recognise their authority. It inevitably results in conflict and gets escalated for resolution. Now, imagine two team

leaders of production & quality in a manufacturing pla[nt] who disagree on the quality standards produced. The i[ssue] having uneconomical standards to meet from [ ] perspective vis a vis the other leader's contenti[on] manufacturing processes need to be revamped to mee[t] standards.

With the matrix structure in place, the two leaders [ ] their bosses in charge of manufacturing & quality at [ ] level. Earlier, it was an emotional conflict, but it gets es[calated] global level. A standout leader at the global level sees the[ ] actual perspective of lack of alignment & collaboration a[nd] a series of actions that help in limiting the current pr[ ] works with the Regional HR in building processes [ ] collaborative decision-making. He also has coaching ses[sions] the two team leaders to help them understand the commo[n] interest rather than the individual goals alone.

The above situation took place in a Pharma MNC with [ ] consulted for an organisation development initiative. Lea[ders] make structural changes to achieve strategic goals and [ ] problems. Changing structures without changing leadership[ ] required to collaborate would not help meet the objective[ ] focus shifts to helping leaders develop collaborative behavi[our] structure change may not be required.

Let me share another situation with you, my esteemed rea[der] the IT industry, it is common for an 'offshore team' head[ed by a] Project Manager based in India to provide services to an [ ] client. Typically, in such a situation, the client is mana[ged] supported by an 'onshore team,' which is the Account Mana[ger] team headed by an Account Manager.

The Account Manager liaises with the client organisat[ion] understand the client's requirements well. After that, he debri[efs] offshore Project Manager to plan how the services shall be del[ivered] to the overseas client. From a hierarchical point of view, the Ac[count] Manager & the Project Manager are at similar levels i[n] organisation. Also, as part of their role, the Account Ma[nager] manages the client account and acts on the client's behalf inter[nally]

between two leaders- both Account Manager & Product Manager. Their goals are not the same any longer. The organisational structure has come between them and the customer's requirements.

While consulting with one of the leading IT companies, we encountered this issue, as enumerated earlier in the scenario. While designing a leadership development program for mid-level leaders in the company, we created a case study for the participants based on the above procedure and asked them to analyse what could be the causes of problems and suggest possible solutions. Their suggestions included the following:

- The two leaders should collaborate.
- Leaders should listen to each other with empathy.
- The Project Management team should consider the Account Management team as their internal customers.
- Understand the internal customer requirements.
- Both leaders should periodically meet the client together.
- Build interpersonal relationships between the two teams.
- Celebrate wins together and applaud each other's successes.
- Set common team goals.

If one were to accept that every person in an organisation needs to have a customer, whether internal or external, most problems like the above would be seen from the correct perspective, and resolution would be faster. Internal customer philosophy has a hugely positive impact on creating alignment in any delivery team. A clear line of sight to the external customer helps teams and organisations identify the next customer. The second aspect, which is fundamental to the resolution of the issue is to be focused on meeting the internal customer's requirements without prejudicing the situation by looking through the prism of hierarchy and ego.

Inter-departmental conflicts are a fairly common scenario in almost every organisation. Conflicts between Operations and Sales, HRD & Finance, Customer Success & Manufacturing Operations, and so on, occur in various organisations. The reason is invariably the internal success measures of one department which may conflict with the success measures of the other department. If the overall success measures of the company are made the focal point, and every department aligns its success measures with the organisational success measures, the alignment internally would improve considerably. This would lead to a far better internal work environment, productivity and performance across all performance indicators. This process of alignment is equally important in a team.

While consulting for a large BFSI company, we met with all the C-Suite leaders to understand their perspectives on the business strategy the CEO had worked on over the last six months to take the company to the next growth level. We were concerned when we realised that the perspective & understanding of the strategy varied widely from one leader to the next. Evidently, there needed to be a more common understanding of the strategy.

The following day, we sought a meeting with the CEO and shared our observations. The CEO was surprised and upset that his leadership team needed to clearly comprehend the new strategy and actions. He informed us that less than six weeks before he had a half-day session dedicated to sharing the strategy. The Chief Strategy Officer and the CEO had taken the leadership team through the new strategy in detail and received their confirmation that they were on board with it.

In a personal chat with the CEO, we helped him appreciate that sharing and informing of a strategy formulated by a different group than the leadership team would ensure understanding but not alignment. In general, alignment entails knowledge, comprehension, commitment, ownership, respect for each other in the team and unswerving loyalty to make it happen. Many years ago, Claus Moeller, Founder of Time Manager International (TMI), coined the term 'teamship' after studying what makes some football teams successful in emphasising the criticality of specific characteristics that can help a group of individuals perform as a team.

Characteristics of winning teams:

1. Each team member brings out their best.
2. Everyone identifies with the vision.
3. Success criteria are shared & the team is organised around its' success criteria.

4. Everyone is willing to change instantly.
5. The team can overcome obstacles.
6. Everyone possesses professional skills.
7. Everyone has relational skills.
8. The team is a "we" team.
9. Everyone learns and shares.
10. The team leader is visible.
11. The team leader helps everyone to achieve success.
12. The team leader enjoys respect.
13. Good performance is rewarded.

We informed the CEO that we wanted to plan an offsite session over two days with the leadership team, where we would let them ask questions and get their input on the entire process. The objective was that the strategy output should be seen by the leadership team as their output and not a third party's. The CEO agreed and the session was facilitated to ensure everybody's full participation and comprehension to create 'our strategy' and not 'CEO's strategy'.

The entire focus of the process followed was to engage as a team and not as a group. I have shared the team development process in the Annexures & it can be used for any team output or for building a strong team culture. The process is based on some outstanding research by Prof. Tony Cockerill of CHPD. We had the privilege of being partners with CHPD in India and used the team process with many clients, resulting in great success. The high-performing leadership behaviours that get deployed in the team development process include:

- Empathy
- Teamwork
- Information search
- Generating ideas
- Innovative thinking Communication

There is a 'WOW' moment in the team development process when you ask the team at the end of Day 1 — 'Whose idea/strategy/plan is the one which is being selected?' The resounding response is 'OURS.' This is when you realise that the individuals have successfully travelled the long path from being a group to becoming a team. In addition, each team member is aligned with the goals & how they would be achieved. Each member knows what the role expected of them is and of each member of the team. There is a spirit of camaraderie between members. Over an extended period by using the TDP, the team would develop all the 15 characteristics of 'teamship' shared earlier.

The core attitude that brings about the transformation is listening. Quite often, we already have an answer to a question before it is asked. We do not ask questions to seek information but to show the absurdity of the idea proposed by the other person. We do not seek clarification, but we pass judgment. We do not build on the ideas of others but propagate our own. Empathy, a core component of listening, is recognised today as the most powerful leadership behaviour and the most required in today's fast changing, dynamic & volatile environment.

I strongly urge you to bring these few questions into your meetings. Over time, you would observe a gradual change in your outlook towards other team members. The process also ensures all team members' alignment with the plan/strategy.

Questioning and probing

- Could you expand on your ideas about . . . ? What do you have in mind when you say . . . ?
- Please could you elaborate on your point regarding . . . ? Sorry, I didn't catch your point on . . .
- Is there anything else in your mind concerning . . . ? What are the reasons for . . . in your opinion? Could you explain why you think . . . ?

Paraphrasing & Summary

- Clarification- what you are saying is . . . In other words . . .
- Are you saying . . .
- Let me see if I understand your point of view . . .

You can quickly deploy the process within your team and in an interdepartmental group with conflicting priorities. The TDP encourages the group members to start working as a team and creates alignment among the team members.

Toxicity & Dysfunctionality

Teams often experience a kind of negativity during team meetings due to arguments, conflicts, poor listening, delays in timelines, emotions swirling around etc. Team discussions become an opportunity to score points over each other, blaming one another, forming sub-teams within the team, and so on. When the scenario of your team meetings has any component of the above, you know that the team is becoming dysfunctional and the air is toxic. So, how does a team leader manage and lead a team that has become dysfunctional? How do we handle such situations where the team cannot function as a 'WE' team due to two or more individuals?

I had the misfortune of experiencing this during the early days of my career. As I shared previously in the book, my first career assignment was in Orissa, where I had taken over the responsibility of the Branch Manager. Before I took over, the operation was handled by a Sales' supervisor. He was vehemently upset by the fact that a new young person had come over to take charge.

Mishra, the Sales supervisor, had experience of over ten years and worked at the Calcutta Regional headquarters before being shifted to Bhubaneswar to start a minimal operation. An agronomist by qualification and training, he knew his basics very well from a technical standpoint. He was most comfortable with farmers, guiding and educating them, but needed more capability on planning sales operations, managing teams and channel partners.

When the business started expanding, I had to recruit new sales representatives. Most of the hires were fresh agriculture graduates. I hired the freshers for their energy, positive thinking and physical capability, as travelling was a primary requirement and their enthusiasm to create something in addition to their technical ability. Within ten months of my joining, I led a team of five sales representatives along with Mishra, as the Sales supervisor & an Office supervisor. The business was growing beyond the expectations of the headquarters and regional headquarters, and I was getting showered with positive feedback from my bosses.

At the time of this incident, I had started observing that Mishra was giving a contradictory view to everything that I was saying at almost every opportunity during team meetings. Given his far superior knowledge of the technicalities of the business and the fact that the sales representatives were from a similar background, I realised that my authority demanded to be improved. With every passing week, Mishra started contradicting me even on matters clearly outside his domain. When I reflect on the situation, I realise my ego was bruised significantly, and Mishra got on my nerves every time he uttered something against me during team meetings.

I decided to have a separate discussion with Mishra and help him understand his role and contribution to the team's goals. The meeting did not go well because Mishra openly questioned my capability and experience to manage the operations. I could not control my emotions and got into an attack & argument with him. The meeting quickly degenerated into a shouting match, and in the heat of the moment, I asked him to get out of my room.

Mishra was utterly perplexed. He stood there for a few minutes to process everything and left the office immediately. I was also taken aback by my reaction, and given the fact I was fifteen months into my first job, I was clearly out of my depth on how to handle the situation. I knew this could blow up into an unwanted situation early in my career. That evening I reflected on everything that had happened to understand Mishra's conduct over the last few months and my responses to the problem.

I realised that for Mishra to be disappointed with the assignment of responsibilities to me as a fresher was a natural reaction for anyone and not necessarily directed towards me. His reactions in the initial stages would have been the same irrespective of the person in my role. Hence, I needed to understand how someone else would have handled the situation better than I was handling it.

I reflected that I needed Mishra to add his experience to the team and his deep knowledge of the state's topography. What I was not doing too well to get his commitment was positioning him to manage his ego and emotions within the team. I needed to ensure that the team regarded him as a team leader and an expert in his field. In the absence of actions on my part, Mishra was trying to do what he could, and I was perceiving it as subordination and disregarding my authority.

The next day, I called and asked him to accompany me for lunch. We conversed about the incident that had occurred the previous day. I told him that I was genuinely apologetic for the way I had treated him. Mishra also expressed his emotions and I listened to him without interruption. I asked him about his opinion regarding the performance of the team. It was the first time I had ever asked him for his point of view. Mishra gave relevant suggestion and slowly, the conversation shifted from a hostile environment to a positive one where we incorporated our ideas and behaved like a team and not opponents.

I requested him to make a presentation of his ideas so that we could get the team aligned with the plan of action. In the process, I mentioned that he was my co-leader in the team and we should be united, not divided. Without further delay, Mishra made his presentation the next day, and I applauded him for his initiative and knowledge in front of the entire team. You can imagine the impact on the whole team— an alignment of the entire team to the goals and plan of action.

The toxicity which had started gaining currency in the team over the last two months had been identified, corrected and hopefully removed forever. This incident paved the way for me to believe quite early in my career that the team's ethos is highly dependent on the leader's behaviour. Hence, if we want the toxicity in the team to be eliminated, the onus is entirely on the leader.

Similar situations are likely to occur in the career of a standout leader. A standout leader is expected to travel on a higher gradient. Hence, situations can evolve where he will lead his ex-colleagues and other people he had reported to during his career. It is human nature that people may not feel positive in that situation. Still, it is incumbent on the standout leader to understand the feelings and emotions of others and create a productive and conducive environment. If the standout leader does not focus on understanding and managing their own emotions and lays emphasis only on the negative emotions of others, the toxicity will worsen and develop into an unhealthy environment.

To ensure that I corrected the team ethos and did not let it generate into a dysfunctional team with toxic undertones, I needed to:

- understand and acknowledge my emotions – what are my feelings and why I am feeling the way I am.
- accept that I made a mistake.
- communicate the same to the affected person/s and apologise.
- accept that as a leader, it is my responsibility to understand the feelings of my team members.
- help & coach the team members to manage their feelings appropriately.
- develop & implement modified rules of engagement within the team.

The above steps are challenging to implement when you are in the throes of swirling emotions within and around you. Hence, the focus should be on developing your emotional intelligence to be a standout leader. Most of the mistakes that I have made in my career were in an environment where my objectivity had become a victim to an emotional storm raging within me as a reaction to a perceived attack.

I continue to strive and manage this even today, although I have come a long way from when the above incident happened. These are certain mannerisms that can become major derailers and brush away all the leadership strengths that you may possess. It is critical to identify these derailers early in life to start managing them effectively. Learning to manage your derailers is one central pillar of leadership development, which helps one become a stand-out leader.

Alignment is an ongoing process. A collaborative & winning team makes the alignment process easier, but alignment on different decisions, action plans and problem-solving still needs to happen.

Over the passage of time, we start assuming that the team is collaborative and well-knit. Hence, the team leader need not ensure alignment. Issues start surfacing over time and lead to fissures within the team. Therefore, wisdom suggests that even in a collaborative and winning team, alignment on major and strategic issues must be ensured.

Key reader takeaways:

- Aligning, collaborating, and influencing are the capabilities for a leader. They can be leveraged to create 'organisational success' as a leader who works 'systemically' or they can be ignored to the peril of creating a siloed organisation with stunted growth.

6

BUILDING MY POWER GRID

In the long walk of living my purpose, it was indispensable to create a solid support base that would help me achieve both personal & professional goals. It would be necessary for the standout leader to have positive relationships with critical stakeholders within the organisation, industry, social circle, government, and every other stakeholder, who could impact living the purpose. In addition to having positive relationships, another critical aspect that could help the standout leader sail through his entire journey would be to develop a powerful personal brand.

The third element that could support a standout leader to live his purpose is performance. If the performance does not align with the purpose, there will be certain substantial hiccups in achieving what the standout leader would wish to achieve. Performance is essential to build a power grid– essential, but not sufficient!

Finally, a standout leader's underpinning of positive relationships is mandatory. Personal brand & performance stem from the behaviours of persuasion, empathy and self-confidence. These behaviours would be the core of the armoury of a standout leader. These are the nutrients that help to create the power grid and strengthen it. One of the earliest things a standout leader should start working on is to create a robust power grid.

The three Ps (performance, positive relationships and personal brand) developed, nurtured, and honed through the behaviours of the fourth P (persuasion, empathy and self-confidence) help create a strong power grid.

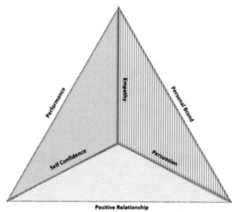

Copyright – Inspireone consultants pvt ltd.

Creating a power grid is a lifelong effort. It cannot magically happen overnight. It takes time to build. Like wine, the power grid becomes stronger and matures with age and time. It is an asset that needs to be nurtured and developed throughout your life. It is the most vital intangible asset you would have created and the highest value amongst all your asset classes– education, experience and physical assets. This power grid can be leveraged at any stage in your life and in many situations. It can create different assets and help tide over situations that threaten your personal & family happiness.

Your power grid determines your value as a professional & a person. The elements of the power grid are interwoven and have a significant bearing on each other. It is not essential that one must be equally good in all the four Ps. You will observe from your observations and experiences that if you excel even in one of the four Ps, there will be a positive impact on the other three Ps. While the first three Ps of performance, positive relationships and personal brand are the assets you create over time, persuasion, empathy & self-confidence are the leadership behaviours that nurture and build these assets.

Performance

There is an aura around a high performer in any social, official, or industrial gathering. That aura is a heady combination of self-confidence and self-belief emanating from a sense of invincibility, which a high performer exudes. The veneer of invincibility has its roots in the knowledge that 'No one can touch me because if I'm not a part of the system from which I have to be removed, the system would be the poorer for that.' The power comes from the confidence of creating value and knowing that everyone is aware of it.

There is a huge difference between having achieved once and having achieved consistently. A high performer is a person who has performed diligently in almost all situations and at different levels, roles etc. There are so many folklores and factual stories about such high performers that it becomes difficult to separate facts from myths.

Narinder was an Area Manager reporting to me as his Regional Manager. I was new in the company and the role at that time. Narinder was older than me and differed in various aspects. He was a favourite of my predecessor, or so I was told by a few people who were perhaps inimical towards Narinder. In hindsight, I was biased against him from the beginning. The initial feedback about him was that he was a bit brusque in his approach with his peers. Unwittingly, my approach towards him became somewhat antagonistic and sharp.

I always found him well-prepared during meetings. His performance on all measures was better than others, if not the best. However, his relations with his peers were a constant red flag as he would constantly bring up issues of non-support and inefficiency of the Service & Spare Parts teams. Not only this, he would always be ready with facts to support his claims of non-performance or inefficiency of others.

As the Regional Manager, it was my job to ensure that Narinder & his team were fully supported by Regional Customer Service & Spare Parts teams, who also reported to me. To my chagrin, I found that his complaints were on the mark, and it began to reflect on my performance as a Regional Manager. I would push Narinder to go beyond his original sales targets to offset the regional shortfall, and he would ensure that he succeeded in doing so.

At the same time, his arrows vis a vis the regional support teams were hitting the bull's eye, and I was feeling the heat. I found myself reacting emotionally and not objectively. I was almost willing to do something wrong to rebuke him strongly. My desire to find Narinder in the wrong made me protective of the Regional Support team. Even if I wanted to take action on his report quality, timeliness, and blatant antipathy towards his colleagues, I could not. His performance on most of the critical business markers was exceptional.

One day, Narinder came to me with a comprehensive report on the different product failures that had taken place in his area in the last six months. The report was of high quality and clearly defined the gaps in our product quality & service. He had gathered information from some of the dealers, spoken to some customers and some of the manufacturing personnel.

In addition, Narinder had also put together a plan to manage the situation on the ground over the next six months until more strategic solutions were identified and implemented. They had also done laid a plan with a dealer's help to see the proposal's practicality. I was undeniably stunned! Narinder had done what was my job! I felt very embarrassed and somewhat ashamed that I was trying to find something wrong with someone portraying such outstanding leadership capabilities.

What saved Narinder from anything unsavoury was his excellent performance. His performance was also a saviour for me with regards to taking a discriminatory action. Needless to say, I gave the project to Narinder so that he could manage it effectively, which he did with great aplomb. His performance earned him plaudits from the Corporate Leadership team for successfully navigating a problem and implementing a solution across functions etc.

Narinder's consistent performance helped him to create a shield against any unwelcome action against him by any stakeholder seeking revenge based on personal prejudices. Narinder created a formidable 'power grid' for himself with his performance. He inspired me on how performance is your best armour against any action adverse to your interest. Performance is accurate and not even the most powerful person in the organisation can fight or create dents against any individual with the credentials of a genuine high performer.

For a standout leader, consistent performance is an absolute necessity and there can be no substitute for it. Narinder's performance made him sought after by his colleagues and superiors and helped him build relationships with various stakeholders. His personal brand as an authentic performer got further embellished. All of this enabled him to develop his confidence. Being a person who loved being with people helped him to strengthen his power grid. From my interactions with standout leaders, I have figured out the following characteristics of a high performer:

- High performers consistently take on more work and leadership tasks. They go above and beyond what their role requires.
- They set their own stretch goals (sometimes apparently impossible ones) and work hard towards achieving them.

- They have a remarkable ability to learn, analyse failures, and solve problems.
- They cross over to the other side and collaborate to achieve win-win solutions.
- They have a conscience to complete what is to be completed.

Positive Relationships with Stakeholders

A vital pillar of the power grid is the relationship capital a standout leader must create. As shared earlier, there is a strong inter-dependency between the three pillars of the power grid. Narinder's performance would not have been possible without building good relations with the other stakeholders– dealers, colleagues and stakeholders from other functions.

As a standout leader, one of the basic expectations is to know your stakeholders. In the early years of my career, it was easy to be stumped by an objection to a proposal raised by a person whose existence you were unaware of. A colleague of mine used to relate an instance when he presented a pricing proposal to his boss for clinching a critical business deal after a great deal of research work. Unfortunately, after a few days, he found an email from someone in the Corporate Costing department with a list of endless questions.

Most of the information were easy to provide, but some were clearly optional. But it slows down the process and makes a person who is very keen to achieve goals lose interest. A standout leader understands the importance of ensuring all stakeholders are fully aligned with the idea the leader wants to promote. He would ensure that he has complete knowledge of the process which would be followed to approve his plan and of the stakeholders who are a part of the process.

In general, the number of stakeholders could be more well-known. A true leader knows the requirements of each stakeholder and how the requirements are to be provided. Hence, the operations usually go on smoothly like a well-oiled machine. Occasionally, an irritable boss checks out if his writ still runs by asking for something out of the ordinary to shake the system. But every leader knows their boss and handles the shaking of the system with aplomb.

However, the scenario changes dramatically when we move from the operational to the strategic arena. This requires a good understanding of the emotional profile of your key stakeholders (including your supervisor), their need for information & how they would like to receive the information. Elsewhere in the book, I have narrated my inability to approve proposals by an inter-departmental group due to the need to ensure that key stakeholders are met before the meeting, and their objections & suggestions are noted & incorporated. This process of alignment must be considered.

So, the ultimate question is— how do you understand your stakeholders?

The capability to understand people & relate or communicate effectively with them is one of the most challenging things to develop. As a Consultant, I once advised the Chairman & CEO of a group on the development of his corporate centre. While going through the list of people he suggested for various strategic roles, I found one name I could not reconcile with the role indicated for him.

Sam, the person being suggested by the Chairman for the Business Head role of an emerging business, was a financial controller in one of the other business units. In my opinion, his experience, age and education were not consistent with the requirements of the role. His experience so far in his career was deep but needed to be wider to take on such a crucial role.

The Chairman listened to my perceptions and suggested that I participate in the quarterly review of the BU in which Sam was the controller. I observed Sam very closely during the three-hour examination to assess his success in the role being considered for him. During the entire period, I found Sam to be very supportive of his colleague's performance by sharing data that strengthened their point of view. He explained the performance variances and suggested additional measures which the colleague could implement to bridge the performance gap.

I observed that even though he had a different point of view, he built on his colleague's point and created an overarching idea that was more innovative. I observed the BU Head involving Sam in crucial business issues and accepting that Sam & he differed on a strategic proposal he wanted the Chairman to approve. The proposal did get approved with some risk mitigation measures suggested by Sam. It became evident to me that Sam had gained the trust of almost all his colleagues. He would support them and share his differences openly and with data to support the same. At the same time, his authenticity was obvious to me. He would be highly objective in his judgment and was looked up to by all his colleagues.

I found Sam to be of mild temperament and not flamboyant. His communication was always optimistic even when he disagreed with something. As a good listener, he displayed strong behaviours of empathy and persuasiveness to get the group together. His positive relationships with his colleagues, supervisor and Chairman were visible to us. This aspect, backed by his performance during his tenure with the group, helped me understand why the Chairman considered Sam efficient.

On our way back to HQ in the car, I complimented the Chairman for his discerning eye and willingness to take the risk with Sam as the BU Head. Sam had never run a line function before in his career, which would be a critical requirement to consider anyone for that role. However, his leadership capabilities were so strong that I was inclined to agree with the Chairman. Eventually, Sam took over the role and ran it well for a few years. His performance was noticed by others outside the group too.

Sam was offered a position, and he took over the job of the Managing Director for an emerging media house, ran it for over twenty years and turned it into one of the leading media groups in the country. I learned from Sam that building positive relationships requires empathy, authenticity and the ability to disagree without becoming disagreeable, a helping disposition and a genuine passion for what you are engaged in. Another vital quality that Sam exhibited was the mutual trust he shared with his stakeholders.

I revert to my favourite trust equation described earlier, which espouses the direct correlation of trust with credibility, reliability and relationship along with the inverse relationship of trust with self-focus. This means that if your focus on self-interest is high, the trust in you would be lower. However, trust would be a positive outcome if your focus is on mutual interest. Sam had the ingredients of credibility and reliability, and he backed them with strong relationships. He was trusted by his stakeholders and was undoubtedly a standout leader.

Something else which I learned over the years was that while the four P s are the core of the power grid, its magnitude and scale are determined by the ambit or area of your coverage. If the purpose is to be fulfilled, then the scope of the power grid must be in sync with your area of intended impact. Thus, if I aim to create an impact through my actions & behaviours within my circle of friends, company, and neighbourhood, then my power grid should be aligned with equivalent coverage. However, if my purpose is to create an impact at a broader level of industry, country, and academia, then my power grid would require to be proportional in coverage.

Personal Branding

In the cricketing world, almost every international cricketer will acquire a label or a moniker by the time they retire. Even in the neighbourhood games, the teams would have openers, innings builders and finishers. With each label, there lies expectations of specific skills and capabilities. It is expected that Sachin will score a century every time and that Dravid 'The Wall' is not expected to get out ever! If Dhoni cannot win the game with a six on the last ball, then one of the all-time great finishers of the game is likely to be stripped of his label.

Similarly, in the corporate world, labels of strategist, deal maker, risk taker, networker, lone ranger and ubiquitous boot licker are used freely. The world of labels grows faster than your career. The labels or monikers are often perceived as a reasonable reflection of a person's behaviour, skills and a projection of how a person would like others to perceive them. These personal labels or monikers, which probably started in your youth and college days, are the harbinger of your personal brand to emerge and evolve in the coming months and years. A standout leader recognises the potential value of a personal brand and works assiduously from an early stage to shape it. One of the most critical aspects of a brand is its authenticity. This is as true for a personal brand as for a product or service brand. Thus, the personal brand cannot be created based on lies or half-truths!

Some of you may recall the scene from the epic Mahabharata when Dronacharya calls out to Yudhishthira to confirm the news of his son Ashwatthama's death. Dronacharya would not believe the news of his son's death unless confirmed by Yudhisthira, renowned for his truthfulness & righteousness- that was the power of the personal brand of Yudhisthira. As the epic states, Dronacharya believed Yudhisthira when he said, "Indeed, Ashwatthama is dead." Yudhisthira covered up his falsehood by saying in an undertone, "Elephant, not human!" This one blemish marred the personal brand of Yudhisthira for all times. Hence, as a standout leader, you must build your personal brand on the authenticity of genuine values, purpose, skills & behaviours as you have identified in your Leadership Capacity Canvas.

Authenticity focuses on what you have like values and skills and not what you would like to project. The excellent part of authenticity is that it percolates and reflects in your performance. Thus, if the performance/behaviour is in accordance with the personal brand as perceived by the stakeholders, it reinforces the personal brand. However, if the performance/behaviour is at variance with the individual brand, you can imagine the impact on your brand, your reliability and consequently, on the trust factor!

Another aspect of authenticity is that all stakeholders perceive your personal brand uniformly. Suppose your team members perceive you as 'Hands-off Manager' and your supervisor sees you as a detail-oriented 'Hands-on Manager'. In that case, there is an element of projection coming through, and the authenticity of the personal brand is under question. Elattuvalapil Sreedharan is perhaps not as widely known by his name as by his personal brand—

E. Sreedharan is credited for changing the face of public transport in India. His power grid is probably created on the nutrients of self-confidence, persuasiveness and based on the mighty edifice of performance. His performance and track record, backed by his self-confidence & authenticity, helped him to create positive relationships. The combination of performance & positive relationships helped create a personal brand– THE METRO MAN!

Once his personal brand was created, it was strengthened by consistent performance & burgeoning positive relationships fed by self-confidence and persuasiveness. As his ambit of enactments kept expanding, so did the reach of his power grid. The significant factors in creating a personal brand are authenticity & consistency– consistency of performance and consistency of actions & behaviours. Typically, these consistent behaviours for a person must be those which are also his strengths. If you leverage these behaviours in your passion and interest areas, you will watch your personal brand shine.

Raghavendra started his career after an average education background as a Relationship Manager with an MNC Bank. He was a good communicator and easily formed relationships with people. His genuine interest in people helped him strengthen his behaviour of empathy even further. He was good with money and sharp with numbers. He had an almost natural flair for the investment market. He shared his approach with the clients so there would be no expectation gap and dissatisfaction. His clients trusted him and made investments as per his advice. His portfolio grew, and so did his development within the bank.

Recognising the capabilities of Raghavendra, the bank transferred him to Singapore to look after the High Networth Individual (HNI) clients. He continued with his approach of avoiding the high-risk, high-return model and ensured his performance was in line with his clients' expectations. His leadership behaviours of empathy, self-confidence and persuasiveness on the larger canvas of the Singapore economy created an exponential performance. In less than two years, he was the leading star performer in the bank. His clients trusted him even when some of his recommendations did not go as expected or when they made losses. He would ensure that they were always optimistic in the reference period. He went on to become the leader of the HNI business for another bank in Singapore with even better success.

Raghavendra pondered over his career and decided it was the perfect time to take an entrepreneurial plunge. By now, he had already acquired wealth for himself and many positive relationships with clients spread across Asia. Furthermore, people looking to source funds for new opportunities were now reaching out to him as one of the critical sources of funding new opportunities.

He took the risk & shifted to the Middle East and started his own Investment Advisory Firm, advising his clients on investment opportunities and managing their portfolios. As his business expanded, so did the team & organisation. His capabilities of forming positive relationships and consistent performance continued to add to his image and he was able to attract the best talent. His network of relationships included people from diverse fields, which gave him information on geographies and industries.

He found many exciting deals where he could invest his clients' money and ensure good returns. Raghavendra had created a multi-million-dollar business in less than ten years and a host of delighted clients. All of this was possible due to his dynamic performance & positive relationships. In the process, he created another asset— a solid personal brand. Now, clients were reaching out to him and his personal brand was driving his firm to newer heights.

Raghavendra had created his 'power grid' on the three Ps of performance, positive relationships & personal brand. He had built it through the application of the fourth P, leadership behaviours of persuasiveness, empathy, self-confidence & clear communication backed by the individual value of authenticity.

Social media in today's world has given a rocket booster dose to personal branding. It can hasten and speed up the process of building your personal brand. It can help you reach out to a broader audience and multiply your relationships through its lightning communication speed. However, for those relationships to become positive, you need the fourth P behaviour. However, if your performance could be more authentic & consistent, the personal brand can be erased at an even faster speed than with which it was created.

Creating a power grid is a major effort for any standout leader. Once built, the power grid can sustain itself and grow with the continuing inputs and fertilisation of the fourth P– persuasiveness, empathy, self-confidence, and communication backed with the value of authenticity. For a leader to build their power grid, the non-negotiable element is the practiced value of authenticity. Hence, for any aspiring leader, there is a great motivation to develop leadership behaviours of empathy, persuasion, self-confidence & communication. These abilities would help you build your power grid, making you shine. The aspect of continuous learning & development is the hallmark of any leader.

Key reader takeaways:

- Consistent performance is essential for the growth of any standout leader.
- If one's performance does not align with their purpose, there will be substantial barriers in achieving the desired goal.
- One must have an impactful personal branding to build authenticity.   .

ANNEXURES

Content of the Annexures:

1. Creating Individual Development Plan
2. Personal EQ Meter™ - EI profile
3. Team Energy Meter
4. Derailers
5. Drivers Develop
6. Leadership Perspectives Workstyles

.

1) CREATING INDIVIDUAL/PERSONAL DEVELOPMENT PLAN

a)

Individual Development Plan	
Plan to develop Leadership Competencies essential for performance as a leader	
Development plan should ensure impact on performance goals (business goals) through the development of the Selected Leadership Competencies.	
Please state the Competencies identified from your 360 degree report,	Desired Outcome
1. Atleast one strength competency that you may want to leverage further. 2. Two competencies that would have emerged as areas of development. Please validate these with your Supervisor	1. (What should change as a result of demonstrating this competency at a higher level of proficiency). 2. How will you know the development on the competency has happened? What would be a clear measure
Strength Competency (to be leveraged further) 1. **Winning Customers** **Behaviours associated with Winning Customers:** To enhance proficiency levels on winning customers / Customer Focus competency Proactively engaging with the client to improve processes, quality of team capability, get a view of future needs. Take client input into account Take decisions giving priority to the client rather than the internal constraints.	Business Outcomes - lead outcomes 1. Establish a process of Proactive reviews of the existing plan and future possibilities. 2. Finalize at least 2 creative / additional models / forums of engagement with customers. • By the _____ With outcomes of : • Identifying potential roadblocks and preplanning to avoid crisis • Recommendations to the client on more effective ways of implementing projects. • Get insight / information on other things the client needs, which Wissen can also be part of or Wissen can pitch for. • Proactively build processes to provide value add to customers on sustainable basis. • Take initiative to improve / new products / solutions which exceeds customer expectation. Lag outcomes: Better client satisfaction scores More business from the client Client referrals

b)

Individual Development Plan	
Plan to develop Leadership Competencies essential for performance as a leader. Development plan should ensure impact on performance goals (business goals) through the development of the Selected Leadership Competencies.	
Please state the Competencies identified from your 360 degree report,	Desired Outcome
1. Atleast one strength competency that you may want to leverage further. 2. Two competencies that would have emerged as areas of development. Please validate these with your Supervisor	1. (What should change as a result of demonstrating this competency at a higher level of proficiency). 2. How will you know the development on the competency has happened? What would be a clear measure

Development areas (to be developed)
 	
 1. **Developing Talent**
 	
 Behaviours associated with the competency
 	
 • Build a high productivity and capability team.
 • Create bench strength for critical roles
 • Release self time from operational / crisis related activities to perform role of :
   • a team builder,
   • Identifying strategic new products / services /
   • process improvements and client engagement
   • Problem solve for high impact recurring problems – eg attrition / hiring right talent
	Outcome: Lead
	 1. Develop team members XYZ and ABC in the following areas _____ by the _____
	
	 2. Develop team members to anchor the review process for identifying roadblocks and problem solving.
	
	 3. Identify development areas for all team members and create development plans with them with clear outcomes. Use other team members as buddys for development.
	
	 Outcomes Lag: (any / some or all of the following)
	
	 XYZ and ABC should be handling identified areas independently by _____
	 Team members able to problem solve at their own level for recurring problems
	 Development plans articulated and completed for all team members
	 Increase in team productivity
	 Decreased Escalations
	 Decreased time spent on crisis.
	 Team being able to function smoothly in my absence.

c)

On-the-Job Learning: 70%

What challenging assignments should you work on to build skills and achieve developmental goals? List the goal number next to each item.

Goal #	Type of assignment (List the actions to be taken)	Measures (e.g. 100% accuracy, feedback)	Time Frame	Review – by whom and when
1.	Target to have 10 – 15 direct reportee's. Target to build at least 3 leaders reporting to me, all of them should be able to manage 8-10 reportee's each.	Cut down number of direct reportees to 10 – 15 by identifying other leaders from the team	8 Months (Aug - 2022)	Supervisor Review should be done on quarterly
2.	Working closely with client managers to understand the future plan and build the team accordingly. Institutionalize the process to have regular (monthly) sync up with client managers to understand the plan. Target should be at least 20% of people in managed T&M	20% of people into managed T&M	Open (Progress on quarter on quarter basis)	Supervisor Review should be done on quarterly
3.	Developing teammates – guiding them instead of doing their work Try to understand their needs though process and guide them to make sure they are making efforts in the right direction. Coaching, input, direction should also be part of the bi-weekly 1-1. Delegate this work, take help from team leaders, HR etc.	Every month spend around 10 mins to find out how much time I am spending in giving instruction vs direction to my candidates.	3- 6 Months	Self review / Supervisor Review should be done on monthly basis
4.	Encourage people to form mutually beneficial alliance to enable change Build strategic and tactical alliance with relevant stakeholders. Find out 2-3 people from the team and guide them to create the process and run it.	Setting up a process where people meet and share the knowledge to understand a bigger picture.	3 – 6 Months	Self review / Supervisor Review should be done on monthly basis

d)

Training/Education: 10%

What specific training, educational experiences, and performance support measures (including online learning) can you use to develop desired skills and assist in achieving the your goals? List the goal number next to each item.

Goal #	Type of Training/Education/Self initiative	Measures	Time Frame (to be completed by)	Review – by whom and when
1	Read books on Learning to negotiate. One of the book name: HBR Guide to Negotiating Using it in live situations wherever needed It will be covered during workshop also. Share the key points with team members also.	20% of our team into managed T&M	3 months	Supervisor
2				
3				

Suggestions on Developing High Performance Behaviours, which can be used in your IDP

CLUSTER 1: THINKING / CREATING STRATEGY

Gathering intelligence, generating ideas and accelerating innovation are the behaviours that make up the creating strategy cluster. These behaviours contribute significantly to an organisation's performance in strategy formation, planning and 'big picture' thinking. The impact of this behaviour deficit is a firefighting style organisation, characterised by uncoordinated initiatives and lack of information leaving it strategically vulnerable.

Gathering Intelligence

Keeping track of new industry developments, best practices, customer needs and sector trends is how leaders stay informed and gather intelligence. Gathering intelligence is about identifying and accessing information to achieve the most effective analysis of issues to drive rapid and informed decision making.

- Look at the latest market research and trend development data. How is your industry changing? What initiatives are taking place in different industries with regards to your area of work? Implement systems so that your people regularly receive this information to drive a culture of proactive information search. Consider setting up regular information sharing sessions.

- Encourage your people to question the information they use to make decisions. For example, how current is the data? How does it compare to other departments and industries? What are your competitors doing?

Generating Ideas

- All great innovations begin with an idea. Generating ideas enable leaders to create new strategies and address core problems and challenges. By stepping back and taking a broad view of issues, successful leaders look for ways to create new ideas, products and services to open new markets and achieve business success.

- By establishing regular brainstorming sessions with your people and others, you will encourage innovative thinking and broad solutions.

- Restructure meetings so that new ideas, data analysis and industry developments are discussed on a regular basis. Vocalising your thinking will give others the opportunity to build on your thinking and also get them to see things from a different perspective.
- Promote a culture of analytical thinking that looks for common themes in data. Draw upon techniques such as SWOT (strengths, weaknesses, opportunities and threats), mind-maps and brainstorming to problem solve and develop new concepts.

Accelerating Innovation

- The ability of leaders to innovate and solve complex problems depends on their ability to see things from more than one perspective. Accelerating innovation is one of the most important and yet one of the most underdeveloped leadership behaviours. Standing back and considering the alternatives and assessing the pros and cons is typical of this thinking. It enables leaders to look at problems through a number of different lenses to identify the best solution.
- Always identify at least three options while solving a problem or developing strategies for business development. Identify the pros and cons of each option before selecting a final one.
- Consistently create alternative plans, strategies, and predict their impact upon your people and organisation. List all the people who are affected by the problem. Analyse the problem from these different viewpoints.

CLUSTER 2: DEVELOPMENT: ENGAGING TALENT BEHAVIOURS

Establishing trust, fostering collaboration, and developing talent are the behaviours that make up the engaging talent cluster. Outstanding leaders seek to understand perspectives, build relationships, and encourage talents of people. These behaviours are essential to improve performance and create an atmosphere of learning.

Establishing Trust

The success of our partnerships determines the success of our business. Managing the expectations of people and stakeholders is critical to achieving success and fostering a culture of trust and partnership.

- Put in place a program of regular events so people across your team get the opportunity to talk about issues, problems, and any proposed changes that they are concerned about in a safe and non-judgmental way.

- Create opportunities to tell your people, colleagues, customers and clients how you feel about issues. By being open, you will encourage them to speak their mind. You will build a rapport and create open dialogues.

Fostering Collaboration

- Best results are achieved when people collaborate with others and promote teamwork. We drive performance by developing teams to share their expertise, explore their strengths, and use their collective knowledge to create new opportunities, innovate, and strategically respond to business challenges.

- Encourage the team to identify joint projects that move them beyond their individual roles into more collaborative working. Your aim is to help the team develop a strong identity, where they understand their individual and collective strengths.

- Encourage your team to pool its knowledge and expertise.

Pair people who you think will work well together to increase the knowledge of their strengths and limitations as a team. Ensure in team meetings you regularly spend time 'working together' to solve issues or identifying future actions.

Developing Talent

- By developing their people, leaders build organisations. Through coaching, feedback, and training they unleash potential and nurture talent and aspirations.

- Constructive feedback offers your peers and others opportunities to reflect upon their performance. Similarly, it is an opportunity for you to understand the impact of your leadership style, how you communicate, and your work attitudes.

- Hold regular one-to-one meetings with your people to review performance, identify strengths and development areas. Give people regular time to develop themselves in any way that they wish.

- Take time out to identify your own strengths and development areas. Find ways to address your own learning needs. Be a role model for people by investing in your own personal and career development.

CLUSTER 3: INSPIRING PEOPLE BEHAVIOURS

Influencing people, building confidence and communicating effectively are the behaviours that make up the inspiring people cluster. Outstanding leaders inspire and excite others. These behaviours relate particularly to building confidence and excitement in a team and are crucial for achieving support for ideas.

Influencing People

Having good ideas is not enough. Gaining support for your ideas and strategies will signal your success. Our ability to influence others can be the difference between a good idea and a great outcome. Leaders influence not simply by using persuasive arguments but through building alliances that enable them to raise the profile of issues and secure support from other people.

- It is important that you truly understand what drives your stakeholders and that you take their perspectives into account when you are outlining the benefits of your ideas. Tap into others' motivations and priorities to introduce new ideas, ways of working, products, and services.

- Encourage your people to do a stakeholder analysis as a part of any presentation or proposal submission. Ask them to view their proposals from others' perspectives— how is this going to benefit them? What may be their objections? Who can we work with? Who are our stakeholders? Who will need to champion this proposal for it to be successful?

Building Confidence

We achieve success when we build the confidence of our people by celebrating our successes and making our stance on issues clear. Building confidence is how we communicate our belief in our own and others' ability to succeed.

- Always acknowledge and recognise the achievements of your team and peers. Ask your people, both individually and collectively, what they consider to be their most significant achievements over the last six months. Celebrate these successes.

- Regularly take the time to inform your team about the future direction and potential success.

- The performance of your team will be influenced by the statements you make (or do not make) about your belief in their success. Consider how you respond in difficult times. Always model confidence by using language that is motivational and positive. Others will follow your lead.

Communicating Effectively

It is easier said than done but effective communication is the difference between being understood and having an impact. Communication is how we share our thoughts and ideas, pitch a new concept and target our audience with energy and enthusiasm.

- Think about how you can engage your different audiences. Embellish your presentations with your relevant evidence, stories and anecdotes to bring to life the information that you are presenting. Make sure the audience What is in it for me WIIFM is addressed.

- Apply the same approach in your written communications. Structure and signpost your documents in a way that will help your reader understand what is being communicated and the significance of it.

- Encourage your people to develop a communication plan as a part of any initiative that they are working on. This plan should identify their key stakeholders, the key messages they need to communicate, the medium and frequency.

CLUSTER 4: ACHIEVING EXCELLENCE BEHAVIOURS

Implementing change, improving performance, and winning customers are the behaviours that make up the achieving excellence cluster. These action-oriented behaviours are how we break down barriers and make things happen. As leaders, it is our responsibility to ensure tasks are structured, plans and ideas are implemented, and we continually improve business performance.

Implementing Change

Taking responsibility for driving initiatives and encouraging a 'I can do it!' attitude is how we create a culture of success. When we are proactive, we enable, drive change and make things happen. This leadership behaviour can be developed through the following strategies:

- Ask yourself— what needs to be delivered by when and by whom? What are the interdependencies of this work? What resources do we need? What other departments need to be involved?

- Become more involved in projects and initiatives. Speak to your manager about new projects or initiatives that are taking place within your team or department and ask to be involved.

- Ensure that you use the fundamentals of project management in your work. This approach will focus on the deliverables of time, quality, and cost. Identify the milestones to know whether you and others are on track, the resources and roles that are required, the responsibilities and specific actions which each person needs to take. A project plan should be regularly updated and discussed at each meeting.

Improving Performance

Achieving our goals is rewarding and motivating. We can be confident that we are providing the best products and services. By creating a culture of continuous improvement, we will seek excellence knowing that we are measuring the right things and that once we have achieved our goals, we will look for new ones.

- Ask yourself and your team to identify how performance can be improved. Identify team, financial, client and customer service improvement goals. Organise data which needs to be routinely collected. Data reports can then be discussed to evaluate performance against targets.

- Think SMART– specific, measurable, achievable, realistic, and timely objectives.

- Consider creating an improvement board that has details of the improvement, initiatives being undertaken and progress against your goals. It is a great motivator for driving improvement.

Winning Customers

Customer focus is more than satisfaction surveys and complaints resolution. It is about partnering with customers and clients to develop new products and services, redesigning delivery systems, and researching future markets and trends.

- Be proactive in your understanding and responsiveness to customer issues. Place customers at the centre of what you do, and inspire this behaviour in others.

- Put strategies in place that will embed this customer-focus across your organisation. Encourage other leaders to see the strategic and commercial value of partnering with customers.

- Establish product or service development labs with your customers and clients. Encourage your people to view your clients and customers as collaborators. Listen to what your clients have to say.

- Research the market for emerging trends and consumer attitudes.

2)PERSONAL EMOTIONAL QUOTIENT METER™

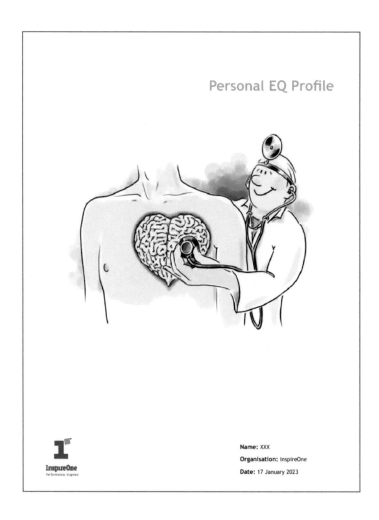

My Overall EQ Profile

Total EQ Score
Emotional Intelligence Quotient

83

0   40   80   120   160   200

What does your score indicate?

The total EQ score indicates the combined score over the 5 main areas and 15 components of Emotional Intelligence. The scores are plotted on a bell curve and the normal range of scores is between 80 and 120.

Group Orientation

Group Orientation is the ability to feel part of one's social group or team and being a co-operative and contributing member. This aspect of social skills has to do with accountability, integrity, trustworthiness, co-operation and collaboration. It involves acting in a socially responsible manner, even though it may not benefit one personally. Group orientation is fundamental for good family relationships, marital relationships, and being a productive and contributing member in one's community and work life.

People with a high level of group orientation:

Are co-operative, contributing and constructive members of their social groups.

Like helping others and avoid exploiting or taking advantage of people. Others frequently depend on them.

Genuinely respect others and their feelings and don't like to see people suffer.

My Score

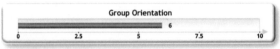

Development strategy:

Try to be a co-operative and contributing member of the groups/teams to which you belong - at work and in your private life.

Be loyal to common group goals.

Speak of your group in positive terms outside the group. Bring up constructive criticism only inside the group.

Defend your group when it is criticised or attacked from outside.

Interpersonal Relations

Interpersonal Relations refers to the ability to establish and maintain mutually satisfying relationships characterised by emotional closeness, intimacy and by the capacity to give and receive affection. It is essential for important managerial competencies like building bonds in the workplace and it is essential for team-based activities and skilful leadership.

People who manage interpersonal relations well:

Are able to establish and maintain mutually satisfying relationships.

Are group oriented, display social participation and, at times, are described as extroverts.

Have positive expectations about interpersonal contact and feel at ease when relating with people.

My Score

Development strategy:

Focus more on people's strengths than on their weaknesses.

Be tolerant. Respect other people's right to be different.

Encourage other people to be their true self.

Inspire people to bring out their best.

Empathy

Empathy is the ability to recognise, understand and appreciate the feelings of others. Being sensitive to what, how and why people feel the way they do. Empathy includes a capacity for interpersonal warmth, involvement, attachment and sensitivity. Empathy is a key component in all forms of interpersonal relations. It is a fundamental social competence vital to work. It is also one of the best indicators of emotional intelligence.

Empathic people:

> Are attentive to emotional cues and listen well.

> Come to the aid of others in response to the needs and feelings they express.

> Identify people's needs for further growth and offer useful feedback.

My Score

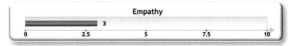

Development strategy:

> Listen to understand - not just with the intent to reply.

> Seek first to understand - then to be understood.

> Do not listen with your ears only. Listen with your eyes and your heart as well. Learn to read between the lines when someone is talking.

> Always be a good listener, no matter with whom you are communicating.

Contentment

Contentment is the ability to enjoy yourself, others and life in general. This contributes to the emotional energy required to get things done. Contented people are pleasant to be with. They are less self-focused, less hostile and abusive and less susceptible to ill health than others. Generally, strength in this area indicates good emotional and social functioning.

Contented people:

Like and accept themselves, which translates into positive self-esteem and self-confidence.

Have the ability to derive pleasure from life. They often feel good and at ease both at home and at work.

Are cheerful and in good mood - it is easy for them to smile and laugh.

My Score

Development strategy:

Take advantage of all the options, possibilities and good moments in life.

List all the things you like to do.

List the people you enjoy being with.

Allocate more time for the things you like to do and that make you happy.

146

Achievement Drive

Achievement Drive is the ability to set and achieve goals, to have a sense of direction in life and to strive to realize your potential. This factor is associated with persistently trying to do one's best and trying to improve oneself in general, which leads to feelings of self-satisfaction. It is an ongoing, dynamic process of striving towards maximum development of one's abilities, capabilities, and talents. Strength in this area leads to a sense of fulfillment beyond materialistic measures of success.

People with high achievement drive:

Have a good idea of where they are going, or want to go and why.

Try to find a sense of meaning in life.

Set challenging goals and take calculated risks.

My Score

Development strategy:

Reward yourself when you have accomplished a goal. Be happy and share your happiness with the people around you.

Actively seek tasks that challenge you to use your potential and bring out the best in you.

Do things that can help you to develop.

Make it a habit to complete the tasks you start.

Optimism

Optimism is the ability to look at the brighter side of life and to maintain a positive attitude even in the face of adversity. Optimism plays an important role in overall self-motivation and is a very important factor in reaching goals and coping with stress. Strength in this area is critical to success in one's private life and at work. Optimistic individuals have drive and motivation that act like an internal engine helping them to persevere despite setbacks, and eventually they succeed because they fully expect to.

Optimistic people:

Operate from hope of success rather than fear of failure.

See setbacks as due to manageable circumstance rather than due to personal flaw.

Are generally motivated to continue even when things get difficult.

My Score

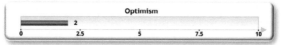

Development strategy:

Try to focus on the brighter side of life. Do not just look at the "holes in the cheese".

Make it a habit to expect the best instead of fearing the worst.

Create and maintain a belief that things will turn out right, and that unfortunate situations can be improved.

Make a special effort to maintain your optimism when experiencing problems and setbacks.

Problem Solving

Problem Solving is the ability to identify and solve daily problems. This skill requires a basic commitment to actively cope with problematic situations in order to improve them. This skill is also linked to a desire to do one's best and to confront problems, rather than avoid them. It includes weighing the pros and cons of potential solutions and foreseeing the possible outcome of one solution over another. It is essential in anticipating and dealing with potentially complex problems on a large scale.

People who are good at problem solving:

Are adept at quickly recognising, defining and solving problems

Push forward and employ a method of overcoming problems, rather than avoiding them

Try to get an overview of the problem before trying to solve it.

My Score

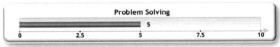

Development strategy:

Try to develop a number of potentially effective solutions to the problem at hand.

Weigh the pros and cons of each possible solution.

Imagine the possible outcome of each possibility, and then make a decision.

Start implementing the solution you have chosen and follow through. If it does not work, try one of the other options.

149

Adaptability

Adaptability is the ability to adjust your emotions, thoughts and behaviour to changing situations and conditions. It involves being open to change, new ideas, challenges and approaches. Individuals who are flexible and deal well with change will fare much better in today's rapidly changing environment. Individuals who are highly flexible have an enhanced ability to adjust their emotions, thoughts and behaviours to changing situations and conditions. They are more likely to meet the demands of any employer in the future and stay employable.

People with high levels of adaptability:

Are open to and tolerant of different ideas, orientations, ways and practices.

Are able to smoothly handle multiple demands, shifting priorities and rapid change.

Can adjust to new conditions and are resilient.

My Score

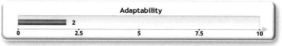

Development strategy:

Learn to welcome change, new ideas and approaches.

Be prepared to change your point of view when new information shows that you are wrong.

When your usual way of doing something does not work, change your strategy and find a better way.

Learn to change before the circumstances force you to do so. When you are forced to change, it is often too late.

150

Self Reliance

Self Reliance is the ability to be independent in one's thinking and actions and to be free of emotional dependency. Individuals and groups with a high degree of self reliance are the free thinkers. Instead of seeing one or two simple ways of doing things, they can see multiple possibilities and are not afraid of taking the risks and failures associated with trying to find a better way. The balance that is necessary to keep this strength in perspective is a sense of humility to avoid arrogance.

People who are self reliant:

Tend to be autonomous in their thinking and actions.

Rarely depend on others to make important decisions or do things for them.

Display a sense of self-confidence and inner strength.

My Score

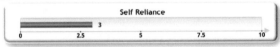

Development strategy:

Have confidence in your own judgement when making important decisions. Do not let others make decisions for you.

Make an effort to be independent of other people's approval or acceptance.

Invite other people to share their ideas and opinions and evaluate them carefully. But, if you feel deep down that doing a particular thing is right, listen to your own conviction - even if others advise you against it.

Impulse Control

Impulse Control is the ability to control your emotions and to resist or delay an impulse, drive or temptation to act. It is the ability to control your anger and avoid abusive, hostile and aggressive behaviour. An important element of impulse control is the ability to withstand adverse events, stressful situations, and strong emotions without losing control. Strength in this area gives the confidence of being able to handle what comes one's way.

People with good impulse control:

Are able to resist or delay impulses and the temptation to act.

Rarely become impatient or have difficulty controlling their anger.

Are generally not loud or too talkative.

My Score

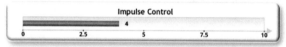

Development strategy:

Learn to control inappropriate, impulsive actions. Do not say or do things that you will regret later on.

Learn to postpone immediate pleasures and temptations. Do not let them keep you from achieving your long-term goals.

Seek actively to manage your emotions instead of being managed by them.

Let your emotions work for you and not against you. Choose the most effective and constructive response to any challenging situation

Stress Management

Stress Management is the ability to actively and effectively cope with stress. The ability to manage stress is a critical factor in dealing with the rapid and constant changes in today's fast moving world. Strength in this area evokes a sense of confidence that one can handle what comes one's way. In a sense, it is the ability to know when and how to act proactively rather than being acted upon. It involves a fair amount of self-discipline that allows one to stay on a task and see it through in spite of difficulty.

People who are able to manage stress well:

Know how to deal with upsetting and unpleasant problems.

Are able to actively do something to improve the immediate situation.

Can handle tasks that are anxiety-provoking or even involve an element of danger.

My Score

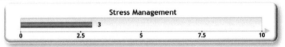

Stress Management

3

| 0 | 2.5 | 5 | 7.5 | 10 |

Development strategy:

List the things, people and situations that are stressful for you (your stressors). Try to include them all.

Be aware of the stressors that are the most difficult for you to handle.

Think of situations that are stressful for you. What happens? Who are you with? Why are these situations stressful?

Be aware of what happens to you physically and mentally when you are feeling stressed. Which signals tell you that you are stressed?

Self Expression

Self Expression is the ability to express emotions, beliefs and thoughts and to defend one's rights in an assertive and non-destructive manner. Self Expression is a prerequisite for effective communication and is an important factor in being decisive. Self Expression means having enough self-confidence and positive self-esteem to be able to stand up for your rights without always seeking approval. This is the self-confidence stemming from one's belief in their own capabilities.

People who are good at self expression:

Are able to outwardly express their feelings, without being aggressive, abusive, arrogant, or defensive.

Can voice views that are unpopular and go out on a limb for what is right.

Are decisive and able to make sound decisions despite uncertainties and pressures.

My Score

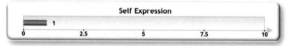

Development strategy:

Learn to express your opinion without hurting others.

Defend your rights without upsetting others.

Learn to express your opinion, concerns, beliefs and values - even when your views are unpopular.

Do not feel ashamed of openly expressing your opinion

Objectivity

Objectivity is the ability to assess the correspondence between what is subjectively experienced and what objectively exists. This involves "tuning in" to the immediate situation, keeping things in correct perspective without excessive fantasising. Strength in this area is critical for good problem solving at home and at work, because it is based on the ability to accurately determine the situation at hand and the course of action to take. Objectivity is about seeing things as they really are, even when the news is not good.

People high in objectivity:

Are often described as realistic, well grounded, and tuned in to their environment.

Are usually good at sizing up the immediate situation.

Maintain focus and avoid losing contact with what is happening around them, even when upset.

My Score

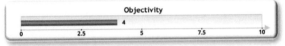

Development strategy:

When making important decisions, consult both your thoughts and your feelings. Listen to your brain as well as your heart.

Actively examine rather than passively assume things. Do not jump to conclusions.

Do not believe in rumours without further evidence. Learn to distinguish between real information and gossip.

Examine the correspondence between what you experience and feel and what objectively exists

Emotional Self Awareness

Emotional Self Awareness is the ability to recognise and understand one's emotions and the way they affect oneself and others. It refers to the ability to differentiate between one's emotions and know what one is feeling, why and what caused those feelings. People who know their feelings are best at navigating themselves through life. They have a more reliable sense of their own feelings in connection with major personal decisions in their private lives and at work.

People with well-developed emotional self awareness:

Know what they are feeling and understand why they feel the way they do.

Realise the connection between their feelings, and what they think, do and say.

Recognise how their feelings affect their performance.

My Score

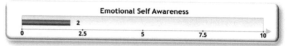

Development strategy:

Learn to distinguish between similar types of emotions like loving and liking, jealousy and envy, hatred and fear.

Feel your emotions as they occur. Listen to your body signals in each emotion: I clench my fists when I am angry, I tap my fingers when I am impatient, I sweat when I am nervous.

Identify your constructive emotions, those emotions which work for you, bring out your best and increase your self-esteem.

Identify your destructive emotions, those emotions which work against you, which are the most difficult to manage and damage your self-esteem.

Self Appraisal

Self Appraisal is the ability to be aware of, understand, accept and respect oneself. It means knowing one's inner resources and one's strengths and weaknesses. Self Appraisal is associated with general feelings of security, inner strength, self-confidence and feelings of self-adequacy. Feeling sure of oneself is dependent upon self-respect and self-esteem, which are based on a sense of identity.

People with well developed self appraisal:

Are aware of their strengths and weaknesses.

Tend to accept and respect themselves and have high self-esteem.

Have a strong sense of self and self-identity

My Score

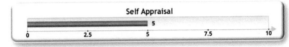

Development strategy:

List your strengths. Include everything that you think you are good at. Don't forget the things that other people notice and appreciate.

Describe each of your strengths as accurately as possible: your attitude, your experience in a particular area and your general and specific skills.

Think of situations in which your strengths have produced good performance, achievements, results or recognition.

Use your knowledge of your strengths to achieve even better results. Put yourself into situations where you can use your strengths.

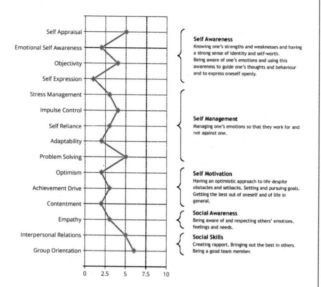

My Detailed EQ Profile

My Scores for the 15 Components of Emotional Intelligence

Self Appraisal

Emotional Self Awareness

Objectivity

Self Expression

Stress Management

Impulse Control

Self Reliance

Adaptability

Problem Solving

Optimism

Achievement Drive

Contentment

Empathy

Interpersonal Relations

Group Orientation

0   2.5   5   7.5   10

Self Awareness
Knowing one's strengths and weaknesses and having a strong sense of identity and self-worth. Being aware of one's emotions and using this awareness to guide one's thoughts and behaviour and to express oneself openly.

Self Management
Managing one's emotions so that they work for and not against one.

Self Motivation
Having an optimistic approach to life despite obstacles and setbacks. Setting and pursuing goals. Getting the best out of oneself and of life in general.

Social Awareness
Being aware of and respecting others' emotions, feelings and needs.

Social Skills
Creating rapport. Bringing out the best in others. Being a good team member.

How to interpret your results:

If the score is below 2.5, this component could be an area of concern. Scores that fall between 2.5 and 7.5 indicate that the component can be taken to the next level. If any score is above 7.5, this component could be a strength that can be leveraged to support you in your work.

Five Areas of Emotional Intelligence

How to interpret your results:

If any bar is below 2.5, this overall area could be an area of concern. Bars that fall between 2.5 and 7.5 indicate that the overall areas can be taken to the next level. If any bar is above 7.5, this overall area could be a strength that can be leveraged to support you in your work.

Intra-personal areas:

These components relate to a person's intrapersonal capacity and pertain to a person's inner self. The subcomponents include: Self Awareness, Self Management and Self Motivation.

Self Awareness	I understand and respect myself. I know how my emotions affect me and others. I can express myself openly.
Self Management	I manage my emotions so they work for me and not against me. I am independent, flexible and effective in dealing with everyday problems.
Self Motivation	I am optimistic and can motivate myself to do my best and achieve my goals.

Inter-personal areas:

These components tap into interpersonal capacity and social functioning. The subcomponents include: Social Awareness, Social Skills.

Social Awareness	I recognise, understand and respect others' emotions, feelings and needs.
Social Skills	I am good at establishing and maintaining positive relationships, and I am a good team member.

3)TEAM ENERGY INDEXATION

reigniting resilience

H.E.R.O. Index

Sno	Parameters	Weekly review on scale of 1-5				
		1	2	3	4	5
1.	New Ideas shared by team members					
2.	Team members' active participation in meetings					
3.	---					

Weekly Trends Analysis

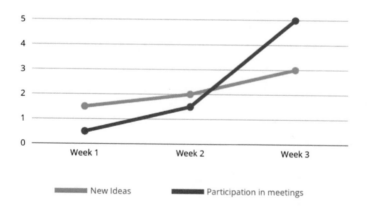

4)DERAILERS

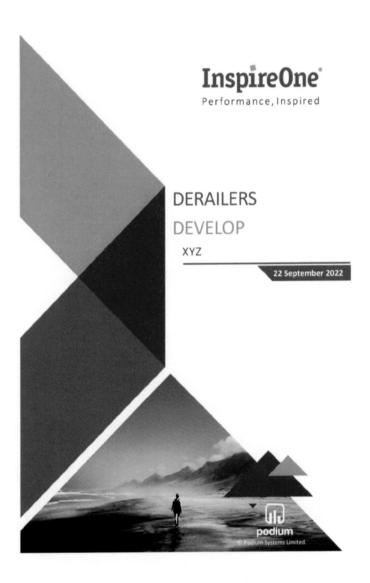

Introduction

 ### The Assessment

The Derailers personality assessment is a measure of a person's propensity for exhibiting limiting behaviours commonly referred to as 'the dark side'. The premise is that traits typically associated with positive performance outcomes can also exhibit counterproductive behaviours.

Derailers was designed to screen for prediction of role performance and identify behaviours that can interfere with interpersonal relationships and prevent individuals achieving their goals. It measures six derailing behavioural areas, all associated with extreme scores on the big 5 personality model.

 ### Private and Confidential

This is a confidential assessment report. It was requested for a specific purpose and has influenced the information and conclusions drawn. The information contained in this report should only be interpreted by a trained professional and in the context of other relevant information (i.e., actual experience, interests, skills, and aptitudes).

 ### Waiver

Derailers is an indicator only. The publishers, therefore, accept no responsibility for selection or other decisions made using this tool and cannot be held responsible for the consequences of doing so.

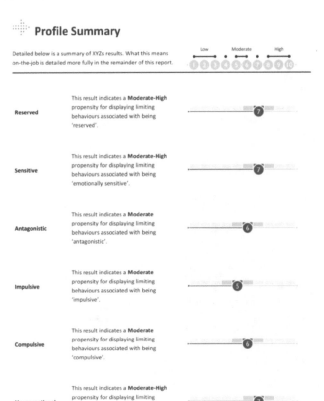

Profile Summary

Detailed below is a summary of XYZs results. What this means on-the-job is detailed more fully in the remainder of this report.

Low   Moderate   High

Reserved

This result indicates a **Moderate-High** propensity for displaying limiting behaviours associated with being 'reserved'.

Sensitive

This result indicates a **Moderate-High** propensity for displaying limiting behaviours associated with being 'emotionally sensitive'.

Antagonistic

This result indicates a **Moderate** propensity for displaying limiting behaviours associated with being 'antagonistic'.

Impulsive

This result indicates a **Moderate** propensity for displaying limiting behaviours associated with being 'impulsive'.

Compulsive

This result indicates a **Moderate** propensity for displaying limiting behaviours associated with being 'compulsive'.

Unconventional

This result indicates a **Moderate-High** propensity for displaying limiting behaviours associated with being 'unconventional'.

InspireOne
Performance. Inspired

5) DRIVERS DEVELOP

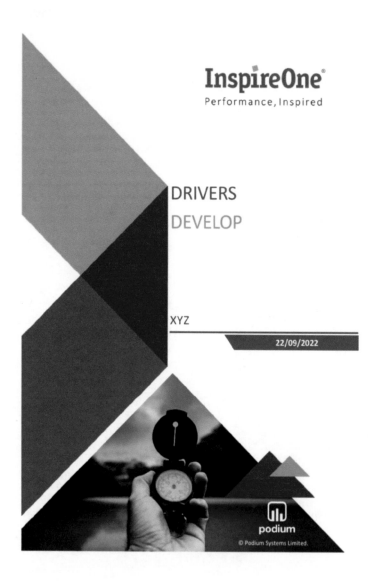

Introduction

This Assessment

Drivers is a measure of personal work values, drivers, and motivations. It considers the aspects of work that are more likely to motivate individuals. It focuses on the eight areas of organisational culture and work motivation identified by Edgar Schein in addition to financial compensation. These areas are detailed below.

Opportunity
The freedom to seek opportunities, take risks and push boundaries.

Security
The need for stability, continuity and job security.

Purpose
The need to use one's talents to help others and make a difference.

Compensation
The need to be well-paid and have significant financial rewards.

Technical Achievement
The need to obtain a feeling of technical accomplishment and work to the best of one's technical abilities.

Stimulation
The need for stimulation, challenge and variety in one's work.

Autonomy
The freedom and discretion to schedule one's work and how the work is carried out.

Authority
The need for power and control over others 'to give directions and instructions to others'.

Work-Life Balance
The need to seek fulfilment in one's personal activities outside of work.

InspireOne
Performance, Inspired

© Podium Systems Limited

DEEPAK MOHLA

Profile Summary

Detailed below is a summary of XYZs results. What this means on-the-job is detailed more fully in the remainder of this report.

Drivers		Lowest Importance Band	Moderate Importance Band	Highest Importance Band
Autonomy — The freedom and discretion to schedule one's work and how the work is carried out.			7	
Stimulation — The need for stimulation, challenge and variety in one's work.			7	
Opportunity — The freedom to seek opportunities, take risks and push boundaries.		3		
Security — The need for stability, continuity and job security.			7	
Purpose — The need to use one's talents to help others and make a difference.			5	
Authority — The need for power and control over others 'to give directions and instructions to others'.		2		
Work-Life Balance — The need to seek fulfilment in one's personal activities outside of work.			7	
Technical Achievement — The need to obtain a feeling of technical accomplishment and work to the best of one's technical abilities.				9
Compensation — The need to be well-paid and have significant financial rewards.		3		

6) LEADERSHIP PERSPECTIVES WORKSTYLES

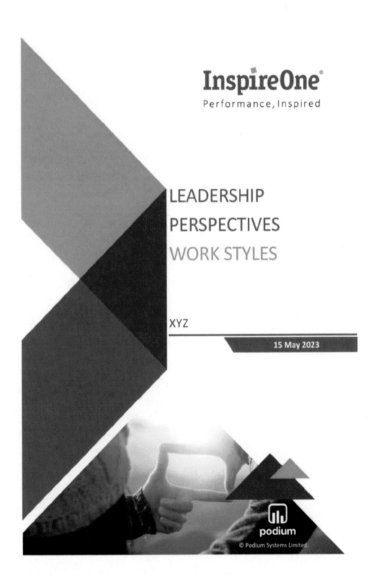

Introduction

The Assessment

Leadership Perspectives - PQ10 is a measure of tendencies and personality preferences and has been developed specifically for online testing.

Leadership Perspectives - PQ10 reflects modern neuroscientific thinking about personality which provides a biological basis and functional structure to one of the most widely accepted models of personality today; namely, the 'Big Five' model of personality. The model provides a hierarchical structure arranged under two broad traits, Plasticity (how people adapt to and engage with the world around them) and Stability (how people maintain stable relationships, motivation and emotional states).

		Big Five Factor	Underlying Trait
Plasticity	**Ideas**	**Openness** *Cognitive stimulation, intellectual curiosity, and creativity.*	**Inquisitiveness** *Intellectual engagement with ideas and challenges.* **Creativity** *Creative and artistic engagement.*
	People	**Extraversion** *Social and behavioural stimulation.*	**Power** *Power, responsibility, and influence over oneself and others.* **Sociability** *Social interaction and engagement with others.*
		Agreeableness *Social stability and social harmony.*	**Compassion** *Empathy, thoughtfulness, concern, and care of others.* **Diplomacy** *Maintaining social harmony and adherence to social norms.*
Stability	**Results**	**Conscientiousness** *Persistence, dependability, and adherence to rules and structure.*	**Drive** *Persistence in the pursuit of long-term goals.* **Orderliness** *Maintaining order, structure, routine, and process.*
	Resilience	**Emotional Stability** *Resilience, confidence, self-belief and composure in response to uncertainty or perceived threats.*	**Emotionality** *Maintaining composure and effectively managing moods and negative feelings.* **Confidence** *Maintaining confidence and self-assuredness in the face of challenges or threats.*

THE STANDOUT LEADER

 Leadership Perspectives: WORK STYLES | XYZ

 The Report

This report provides an overview of XYZs likely behaviours as they relate to different work contexts such as conflict resolution, leading others, and working in a team. The potential strengths and challenges of each preferred style is also discussed.

This is a confidential assessment report. As such, the information contained in this report should only be interpreted by a trained professional and in the context of other relevant information (i.e., actual experience, interests, skills, and aptitudes).

Leadership Perspectives is an indicator of behaviour and preference only. The publishers, therefore, accept no responsibility for selection or other decisions made using this tool and cannot be held responsible for the consequences of doing so.

⊙ **Rating Scale**

Charts in this report are described in terms of a standardised Sten score that is presented on a scale of 1 to 10. As a guide, scores of 1 to 3 indicate a strong preference for the left side of the scale, while scores of 5 to 6 indicate a neutral preference for either end of the scale, and scores of 8 to 10 indicate a strong preference for the right side of the scale.

Scale Ranges

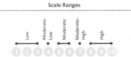

InspireOne
Performance, Inspired

© Podium Systems Limited.

169

DEEPAK MOHLA

 Executive Summary

Detailed below is a summary of the potential strengths and challenges that can be inferred from XYZs assessment results.

Potential Strengths	Potential Challenges
Ideas	
• XYZ should be reasonably adept at making decisions that combine what has worked well in the past with an openness to new ways of working. • She is likely to have a strong operational focus and concern herself with common-sense solutions.	• XYZ may need to discipline herself to keep an open mind to new ideas. • She may get so focused on the here-and-now and not look beyond the obvious.
People	
• XYZ is as likely as most to appreciate a workplace that offers scope for social interaction. • XYZ is likely to relish a position that offers scope for influence and responsibility. • Much more compassionate than the average person, she is likely to put others' needs ahead of her own. • XYZ may be prepared to occasionally speak her mind and encourage tough debate.	• XYZ may build relationships more smoothly with some people and groups than others. • Her strong need for influence may stifle the input of others. • She may get overly focused on what people think and come across as being too soft-hearted. • XYZ is more likely than others to criticise and create disharmony.
Results	
• She should be mindful of the goals she wants to achieve, without needing to strive for them at all costs. • She is likely to approach work in a planned and organised way and set high standards for herself and others.	• She may not always approach tasks with sufficient urgency. • She may be overly dependent on rules and structure and dislike normal, everyday clutter.
Resilience	
• XYZ is likely to manage her frustrations and emotions as well as most people. • She appears as confident as most others and should back herself to handle most challenges.	• She may over-react under prolonged pressure. • She may sometimes dismiss past problems, rather than see them as opportunities to learn.

 InspireOne
Performance, Inspired

© Podium Systems Limited

170

Conflict Styles

Conflict Styles describe the preferred style XYZ is likely to adopt in mediation and negotiation situations. Each style can be described in terms of how individuals relate to and cooperate with others (Agreeableness), and how they take charge and assert themselves (Extraversion). Effective conflict resolution is contextual and the most effective negotiators are able to adapt their style according to the situation.

Primary Style: Collaborating

Individuals who adopt this approach are likely to combine both assertive and cooperative styles. Often high profile team members, they will work with others towards finding a win-win solution that satisfies everyone's concerns. Adopting this style can facilitate more open discussion, a more equal distribution of tasks, and more creative brainstorming of solutions.

Best Contribution	Potential Challenges
• When maintaining the relationship is as important as the issues at hand.	• This approach requires a shared commitment from all parties to look for a mutually beneficial solution.
• When consensus and commitment are valued and trust is high.	• It may not be appropriate in situations where a fast decision is required and time is short.
• When each party is relatively equal in status or when the most powerful party supports a win-win collaborative solution.	• It may require more time and a concerted effort from both parties to achieve a win-win outcome.
• When the solution is dependent on both parties working together.	• Overuse of the collaborating style can lead to feelings of disempowerment and a loss of initiative.
• When both parties have objectives that are too important to compromise.	• To reach consensus typically requires a high degree of trust among all parties.
• When there is sufficient time to resolve each issue in turn.	

Conflict Styles Table

The following table ranks each conflict style according to how well it fits XYZ's profile. XYZ's preference for each style is determined by her agreeableness and extraversion.

	Conflict Style	Description	Supporting Behaviours	
			Agreeableness	Extraversion
1st	Collaborating	These individuals strive to collaborate with others in an effort to resolve conflict.	High	High
2nd	Competing	These individuals adopt a competitive stance when dealing with conflict or negotiations.	Low	High
3rd	Accommodating	These individuals are likely to accommodate the needs of others.	High	Low
4th	Compromising	These individuals adopt a balanced approach to resolving conflicts.	Moderate	Moderate
5th	Avoiding	These individuals tend to avoid addressing conflict directly.	Low	Low

The following terms are used to describe how each style is associated with the supporting behaviours.

High	Moderate	Low

The following colours are used to reflect how closely XYZ's profile matches the supporting behaviours.

Strong   Partial   Weak

Leadership Styles

Leadership Styles describe the preferred style XYZ is likely to adopt when managing/leading others. Leadership Styles are based on the Leadership Grid developed by Robert Blake and Jane Mouton. Each style can be described in terms of how it relates to two behavioural dimensions, people-orientation and results-orientation. Effective leadership is contextual and the most effective leaders are able to adapt their style according to the workplace factors and the team they are leading.

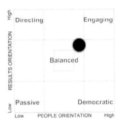

Primary Style: Engaging

Engaging leaders are results-driven and energise others; keeping staff focused on the desired end goal. They motivate with positivity and connect with others by active listening. Engaging leaders rely on their influencing skills to achieve their stated goals and are authentic in their communication and behaviour. They empower, develop and enable staff, and take a genuine interest in their lives.

Best Contribution	Potential Challenges
• When there are multiple stakeholders whose needs have to be balanced.	• This style may undermine team culture as a consequence of group efforts being too thinly spread.
• When the organisational culture supports staff negotiating with managers to identify the best approach to projects.	• Staff may be unable to fulfil commitments made to various parties or stakeholders.

 InspireOne
Performance, Inspired

Leadership Styles Table

The following table ranks each leadership style from highest to lowest according to how well it fits XYZ's profile. XYZ's preference for each style is determined by her people orientation.

	Leadership Style	Description	Supporting Behaviours	
			People	Results
1st	Engaging	Engaging leaders are results-driven and attempt to influence others and motivate them to achieve their objectives.	High	High
2nd	Democratic	Democratic leaders are concerned with encouraging group participation and building consensus.	High	Low
3rd	Directing	The primary concern for directing leaders is to achieve results.	Low	High
4th	Balanced	These leaders balance the team's needs with delivering objectives.	Moderate	Moderate
5th	Passive	Passive leaders give their team the latitude and freedom to make their own decisions and manage their own deliverables.	Low	Low

The following terms are used to describe how each style is associated with the supporting behaviours.

High	Moderate	Low

The following colours are used to reflect how closely XYZ's profile matches the supporting behaviours.

■ Strong	■ Partial	■ Weak

Team Roles

Team Roles describe the preferred roles XYZ is likely to adopt when working in a team. Effective teams require a diverse range of roles to suit the team's objectives and complement one another.

Primary Role: Driver

Drivers are self-directed and passionate individuals who have a strong need to get things done. They are primarily concerned with setting objectives and ensuring deadlines are met.

Best Contribution	Potential Challenges
• Shaping the way in which team effort is applied.	• Getting frustrated with slow progress.
• Directing group activity towards the achievement of critical outputs.	• Being intolerant of less driven or indecisive team members.
• Ensuring the team is not distracted by non-essentials.	• Being too self-centred.
• Keeping focused on the bottom-line.	• Assuming more authority than the position warrants.
	• Striving for results without an appropriate concern for team morale.

Team Roles Table

The following table ranks each team role from highest to lowest according to how well it fits XYZ's profile. XYZ's preference for each role is determined by her capacity to work with ideas, people, and results.

Team Role	Description	Supporting Behaviours		
		Ideas	People	Results
1st Driver	Results-orientated individuals who drive team performance.	Low	High	High
2nd Team Builder	People-orientated individuals who foster team spirit.	Low	High	Low
3rd Implementer	Dutiful and detail-conscious individuals who are concerned with meeting standards and deadlines.	Low	Low	High
4th Coordinator	Assertive individuals who coordinate ideas, resources, and clarify goals.	High	High	High
5th Observer	Detached individuals who prefer working independently of the team.	Low	Low	Low
6th Planner	Systematic individuals who turn ideas into plans and actions.	High	Low	High
7th Networker	Communicative and optimistic individuals who look for opportunities and build contacts.	High	High	Low
8th Innovator	Creative individuals who enjoy exploring innovative solutions and opportunities.	High	Low	Low

The following terms are used to describe how each role is associated with the supporting behaviours.

High		Moderate		Low

The following colours are used to reflect how closely XYZ's profile matches the supporting behaviours.

Strong   Partial   Weak

InspireOne
Performance, inspired

Appendix: Higher-Order Profile

Detailed below is a higher-order profile summary of XYZ's stability, plasticity and big five scale results. Use this profile to gain a higher-level understanding of XYZ's results.

Scale	Description	Low — Moderate — High
		1 2 3 4 5 6 7 8 9 10
Plasticity	**Plasticity reflects the need for reward, stimulation and engagement. Higher scorers seek to explore new goals, relationships, and ways of interpreting the world.**	4
Openness	Openness reflects cognitive stimulation. Higher scorers are curious, value creativity, and seek novelty and variety.	2
Extraversion	Extraversion reflects one's need for social and behavioural stimulation. Extroverted individuals tend to be socially confident and may seek influence over others.	7
Stability	**Stability reflects a tendency towards self-regulation. Higher scorers are less prone to impulsive behaviour.**	6
Agreeableness	Agreeableness relates to one's concern for social stability or social harmony. Agreeable individuals value cooperation over conflict and are compassionate towards others.	7
Conscientiousness	Conscientiousness describes motivational stability or persistence in the pursuit of long-term goals and adherence to rules. High scorers have a strong preference for planning, structure, attention to detail, and goal setting.	7
Emotional Stability	Emotional Stability refers to how people maintain emotional defences in response to uncertainty and threats. It includes concepts of resilience, composure, confidence, and freedom from self-doubt.	5

InspireOne
Performance, Inspired

Appendix: Underlying Traits

Detailed below is a summary of XYZ's underlying trait scores.

	Left Description	Strong Preference · · Neutral · Strong Preference	Right Description
		① ② ③ ④ ⑤ ⑥ ⑦ ⑧ ⑨ ⑩	

Ideas

Openness

Conventional	⑤	Inquisitive
Values tradition and learns from the past; respects the status quo.		Values experimentation; open to change; enjoys intellectually demanding tasks.

Pragmatic	①	Creative
Pragmatic, realistic, and down-to-earth; literal and may prefer common-sense solutions.		Imaginative; looks beyond the obvious; may dismiss practical ideas.

People

Extraversion

Subdued	⑨	Empowered
May prefer to follow; may prefer to support than lead; may avoid responsibility.		Happy to lead; takes charge; may be assertive and controlling.

Reserved	⑤	Sociable
Private; may prefer own company; may avoid the spotlight.		Outgoing, lively, socially confident, and participating.

Agreeableness

Indifferent	⑧	Compassionate
Unsentimental; inwardly focused; may not readily show empathy for others.		Empathetic, caring, and compassionate; thinks about others' needs.

Tough-Minded	④	Diplomatic
Forthright, direct, and straight-forward; may challenge others.		Discreet, restrained, and conforming; careful to maintain harmony.

Results

Conscientiousness

Relaxed	⑥	Driven
Relaxed; tolerant of distractions; able to separate one's work and personal life.		Ambitious; hard-driving; may find it difficult to relax.

Unstructured	⑦	Orderly
Less concerned about rules, process, and planning; may cut corners.		Dependent on rules, process, and structure; likes order and routine.

Resilience

Emotional Stability

Sensitive	⑥	Composed
Emotionally sensitive; actively seeks to eliminate perceived threats.		Emotionally stable and steady; rarely flustered; calming.

Apprehensive	⑤	Confident
Apprehensive; tends to be self-critical; may dwell on past mistakes.		Self-assured; rarely dwells on mistakes; may be overly confident.

InspireOne
Performance, Inspired

ABOUT THE AUTHOR

Deepak Mohla is the Chairman & Managing Director of Inspireone Consultants & Chairman of Inspireone Technologies. With nearly fifty years of diverse experience, his career spans corporate roles, consulting, leadership development, and coaching. An MBA graduate from the Faculty of Management Studies, Delhi, and a Chemistry (Hons) graduate from the University of Delhi, Deepak has demonstrated an enduring commitment to innovation and experimentation.

He began his career at Rallis India, a Tata Group company, and later held leadership roles at Escorts and Modi Xerox, where he left significant marks through his novel strategies and pioneering business practices. His last corporate stint was with Modicorp, supporting Dr. B.K. Modi in creating a strategic-level holding company.

Transitioning from sales, strategy, and general management to human resources, Deepak founded his People and Organisation Development Consulting company, Inspireone Consultants. Partnering with TACK TMI, Inspireone has influenced over 400 organisations and 200,000 individuals, with clients including Tata Motors, Unilever, and Airtel among others. Deepak personally focuses on Senior Leadership Development and Organisation Change and is recognised as a coach, consultant, and innovator. He and his wife Neeta have two sons, two daughters-in-law, and three grandchildren.